PacMan

PacMan

Behind the Scenes with MANNY PACQUIAO—the Greatest Pound-for-Pound Fighter in the World

GARY ANDREW POOLE

Da Capo Press
A Member of the Perseus Books Group

Editorial production by the Book Factory.
Interior design by Cynthia Young in 11 point Sabon.

Library of Congress Cataloging-in-Publication Data

Poole, Gary Andrew.
   PacMan : behind the scenes with Manny Pacquiao—the greatest
      pound-for-pound fighter in the world
         p. cm.
      ISBN 978-0-306-81949-0
      ISBN 978-0-306-82016-8 (International Paperback Edition)
      1. Pacquiao, Manny, 1978–   2. Boxers (Sports)—Philippines—
Biography.   I. Title.
GV1132.P25P66 2010
796.83092—dc22
[B]

                                              2010032912

First Da Capo Press edition 2010
Published by Da Capo Press
A Member of the Perseus Books Group
www.dacapopress.com

Da Capo Press books are available at special discounts for bulk purchases in the U.S. by corporations, institutions, and other organizations. For more information, please contact the Special Markets Department at the Perseus Books Group, 2300 Chestnut Street, Suite 200, Philadelphia, PA 19103, or call (800) 810-4145, ext. 5000, or e-mail special.markets@perseusbooks.com.

10 9 8 7 6 5 4 3 2 1

For Leslie

CONTENTS

PROLOGUE: HOLLYWOOD

AS MANNY "PACMAN" PACQUIAO saunters out of the locker room at the Wild Card Boxing Club in Hollywood, California, he holds out his hand, and a member of his entourage slaps a comb in it. Looking in one of the gym's many grimy mirrors, Pacquiao combs his jet-black hair, brushes off his goatee, and nods his head in self-approval. Someone slips on his watch—a gold Rolex Yacht Master—and then gives him his diamond stud earring, which he puts in his left ear. The champ is ready. Several of us walk down the "secret" back way, out of the boxing gym, where a horde of fans lie in wait with cell phones and cameras. "Manny, just one picture, *pleeeeeaaase*!"

Pacquiao smiles brightly for a moment, but he pays the fans little attention except for a "hello" in the sing-songy way that Filipinos extend an English word's last syllable. He gets ushered away. Pacquiao's burly security detail apologizes to the fans, "Sorry folks," and then roars, "We have to keep it moving!" The champ is hungry.

Pacquiao is going only about forty feet away, but there is enormous urgency. It is time for the champ's dinner. Sometimes he spars for thirty rounds. During training he eats five times a day, and if he doesn't get enough food the world goes haywire. (Pacquiao has trouble getting up to his new fighting weight of 147 pounds and has said that the consistent food intake can be exhausting. "I was miserable when I was in the lighter weights, and I am miserable now," he laughs.) After pressing through the crowd, he jams his way into Nat's Thai restaurant, his regular nightly spot. The place has orange walls and red curtains, which eager fans are always trying to peer through to get a glimpse of the world's greatest boxer. Alex Ariza, Pacquiao's strength and conditioning coach, has already ordered dinner. It is the same at every meal night-after-night: Filipino dishes of beef, chicken, fish, soup, and rice. Spending the last four hours training harder than any athlete alive, Pacquiao lets out a deep breath and sits down at the table. The whole dinner is choreographed. The restaurant's owner dramatically pushes PLAY on a remote and suddenly, the enormous flatscreen television facing Pacquiao lights up, showing a replay of one of his fifty-six professional fights. Unfolding on the screen is Pacquiao versus Jorge Eliecer Julio, circa 2002, before the PacMan's popularity went global. It is an undercard clash out of Memphis when Pacquiao was eight years younger than he is now. He had ridiculous frosted hair, a wispy mustache, and weighed 120 pounds—almost 25 pounds less than what he weighs now in 2010. After Julio hits Pacquiao with an elbow and a low blow, the announcers talk about how Pacquiao's sense of sportsmanship is so deeply ingrained that he refuses to resort to dirty tactics. In the corner, between the first and second round, Pacquiao's trainer, Freddie Roach, tells him to go at Julio with a left hand after a double jab. Off the stool, Pacquiao does just that, and seven seconds into the second round Julio eats Pacquiao's left glove and falls to the canvas. Julio's brain has sporadic communication with his body.

Pacquiao hunts him. Thirteen seconds later, Julio gets dropped again. Pacquiao relentlessly pounds his helpless opponent, and the referee mercifully stops the fight. Pacquiao, the one sitting across from me in the restaurant, studies the replay on the flatscreen, raises his eyebrows a couple of times, and smiles. The puckish grin can change the mood of any room. It can brighten the day of a sick child or a president of a country. His tablemates see it and everyone laughs. There doesn't seem to be a shred of malice in him. A big part of Pacquiao's success, like that of Muhammad Ali's, comes from his ability to enjoy himself. Although he has grand ambitions—like detailed plans on helping the rural poor of his country—many of his outward actions resemble that of an immature prankster. One of his favorite practical jokes at Nat's is sneaking a fork into his guest's jacket. Then he has the restaurant owner catch the person "shoplifting" the silverware. The whole entourage knows it's coming and looks at the guest with mock seriousness and shame. Pacquiao smiles and laughs. They've seen it a million times, but they still laugh.

As the food is brought to the table, ten members of his entourage mosey in for dinner. Everyone has cheap cell phones, and they're checking text messages, occasionally looking up to chit-chat with one another. Pacquiao's on his BlackBerry, frantically checking NBA scores (he gambles a lot on basketball). The restaurant in a rundown strip mall is crowded, and the excitement of the exclusively Filipino crowd inside is off the charts. Ninety million of their fellow countrymen would die to be so close to the national icon. These lucky couple dozen people can't always contain themselves because they are close to the Inner Sanctum of Manny Pacquiao. Nat's is as much a Filipino tourist stop as the Hollywood sign. With Pacquiao's $700 per day patronage, the restaurant thrives. The other Filipino diners, who often just tell the owners to charge Pacquiao for their food, come over and plead for an autograph, and they nudge Ariza, a muscle-bound Latino, out of the way so they can sit next to their idol. Pacquiao sees it as a necessary part of his fame. A heavily made up, middle-aged Filipina pesters Manny to endorse some sort of magical bracelet, and a woman—a friend from his childhood—from his hometown of General Santos City sits across from him. She whispers to me, "He is the same Manny. Even more humble now." They laugh about old times. It is thought that Pacquiao probably suffers from attention deficit disorder (ADD) because he repeatedly shows intensity for a few minutes—the length of one round—and then he is on to something else. Pacquiao slurps some *tinolang manok*—the chicken-broth soup with special leaves from his native Philippines that he eats at almost every meal and which has bulked him up through seven different weight divisions, all of which he has dominated. At five feet six and 145 pounds, he is the greatest and unlikeliest pound-for-pound fighter in the world. "The sodium helps him retain water," points out Ariza. Pacquiao is constantly asking his Filipino buddies to bring *malunggay* leaves, often sneaking them through customs, so the soup's flavor is just right. Dishes are brought out one after another: beef, shrimp, rice, always rice.

When someone wants Manny's attention, they yell, "Pacquiao!"

Mike Tyson is on the phone.

"Pacquiao! It's Mike Tyson. He would like to talk to you." And a phone is handed to him. Pacquiao seems pleased, but just about as pleased as he would be talking to the woman from his hometown. So many people want a piece of him. A few of the people around him, the people who really care about him, whisper about how his trust will bring him personal and financial ruin. The stories of his financial burdens have become legendary within his circle. Everyone takes from Manny Pacquiao, people tell me constantly. Two people that day have told me that Manny—who *Time* magazine named one of the world's most influential people last year—gave an entourage member a large sum to hold for him for a few days, and the man turned around and gambled it away. Executives at Fortune 500 companies hand deliver checks to him because they worry that Pacquiao's entourage might pocket the money. Pacquiao takes a philosophical view of the thievery around him, telling me that God has given him bounty and who is Manny Pacquiao to not give God's blessing away? When their time comes, he says, the men will face God.

"Hi Mike, yes, yes, call me at my home number. Nice to talk to you, Mike."

Pacquiao's face is a little blotchy from sparring. His body is good and sore. His right hand aches. Ariza wraps it in an ice gel. Melon is brought to Manny. This is a typical Filipino meal: In the southern Philippines, from where he hails, the diet consists mostly of rice, fresh fish, and different fruits—watermelon, dragon fruit, and melon. He eats while he gets wrapped, and he talks on the phone. Ariza makes him a pink-colored protein shake, one of three he has each day. Manny downs it.

The television starts on the karaoke. Manny complains about his hand, which is probably sore from hitting his sparring partners so hard. Alex tries to stretch it a little and Pacquiao grimaces in pain. He doesn't want anyone to see his anguish, and he looks hard at me, daring me to write about it. Manny's personal photographer brings in a photo and shows it to him. It is a large photograph of Manny and Julio Caesar Chavez. "My idol," says Manny. His eyebrows rise playfully, and he laughs. Manny has a lot of idols. Manny wonders where his photographer is getting the poster-sized pictures. "I bought a printer, they cost $60,000, but I got the earlier model, it's cheaper, but . . . but that's why I am broke." Manny handpicked the photographer out of the Wild Card's crowd one day. The man had taken a day off from his construction job to come to the Wild Card and take photos of fighters walking in and out of the gym. Pacquiao perused some of the photos on his cheap camera, liked what he saw, asked him if he wanted to be his personal shooter, then went to Samy's Camera and bought him $20,000 worth of camera bodies and lenses.

"I have one of those printers in the Philippines," says Pacquiao. "The ink is very expensive."

Ariza rolls his eyes then flicks Manny in the thigh, and Manny returns fire. They are like two rambunctious kids. There is a Boston Celtics fan at the table, and Manny starts teasing him. Manny loves basketball, plays it obsessively. Like many Filipinos, it is his favorite sport. He is a Celtics fan, too, ever since he fought Miguel Cotto, and Kevin Garnett and the rest of the Boston team joined him in his post-locker room celebration. Other athletes revere Pacquiao. But Pacquiao exudes humility. That night he bowed his head and shyly asked the six foot eleven Garnett if they could take a photograph together. Since Pacquiao spends so much time in Los Angeles, he doesn't broadcast his Celtics allegiance too much, and he even has a Lakers license plate holder on his black SUV.

People keep coming in and bumping Ariza aside so they can get a photo with the champ.

"This is dinner, not a photo shoot," says Ariza, perturbed.

Manny is distracted but accommodating, curling the thick fingers of his left hand around the people to get closer to them. He starts singing karaoke. He takes calls and signs photographs.

"She calls out to the man on the street . . . ," he sings the Phil Collins song. It's 6:15. "It's cold and I've nowhere to sleep . . ."

Alex, putting his forefinger to his temple, acts like he is shooting himself. Alex and Manny are close, and a lot of the yes-men don't like him. Ariza, a native of Bogotá, Colombia, has a lot of newfangled ideas. Most of the people in Manny's entourage are from down home in the Philippines' southern provinces. Ariza spends his time studying exercise physiology risk-benefit charts to give Manny an edge; they believe hitting Manny in the stomach with a bamboo pole is what really strengthens their boss. Ariza turns to Manny with a serious expression, "Manny, I need to ask you. Manny, I am serious, I need to ask you something: Are you going to run tomorrow?"

"I have to run," he says as he raises his eyebrows. Pacquiao fakes a serious expression. He won't take his eyes off his BlackBerry, which irritates Ariza.

"If you run, there will be an elevation in your glucose. They always tell you not to do anything before the test." (Pacquiao will be taking a pre-fight blood test for a fight against Joshua Clottey, and Ariza wants the test to go smoothly.) "I'm trying to help . . ."

"Freddie wants me to run."

"No he doesn't. One hundred percent, he doesn't want you to run."

"Have him BBM me." Pacquiao's voice tends to squeak in English, and he gives his mock serious expression again, which irritates Ariza.

"*What?*"

"BlackBerry Messenger me." Manny laughs, looking away from his BlackBerry and winking at me. It is doubtful that Freddie Roach, his old-school trainer, has ever BBM'd anyone. Ariza is growing more serious. Manny Pacquiao likes to stick to virtually the same training routine, but he has let Ariza, who boasts a lot of modern training techniques, into his circle. Everything that goes into Manny's mouth, every run, sparring session, plyometric workout is finely tuned by Ariza, consultants at UCLA and San Diego State, and a nutritionist who is a devotee of Bruce Lee. Ariza is anal about his fighter, who tends to work too hard and not always listen when he tries to get him to slow down.

"I'm going to talk to Freddie right now." Ariza is usually a calm presence and a charming fellow, but he is pissed. He storms upstairs, conferences with Roach. He returns with a phone and hands it to Pacquiao.

Freddie Roach, who is considered by many to be the best trainer in the world, is on the line. He tells Pacquiao not to run tomorrow. Pacquiao listens, nods sagely, and then hangs up.

"You win," says the PacMan.

"You guarantee me—100 percent—you *won't* run?"

"I promise."

Manny turns back to the karaoke, bobbing his head as he sings, "I can tell by your eyes. . . . If I can see you just a little bit longer."

The whole table—sycophants, relatives, a couple pretty girls who have appeared out of nowhere—sings. Despite his crackling high-pitched voice, Pacquiao has sold millions of records in his native country. "Us Filipinos are good singers, we have good voices," says a man sitting next to me. He looks at Manny to make sure his boss is listening. "Manny has a good voice." Everyone starts talking again until the opening lines of "Hotel California" appear on the screen. "Welcome to the Hotel California," Pacquiao croons.

Pacquiao, like a little boy, holds a microphone. He has a photographic memory, learned to play the piano in one week, and, when he is not training, often sleeps only three to four hours a day. He is lost in the song. His eyes are raised as he reads the lyrics. He has a goofy expression. "Manny is mysterious but transparent," someone told me once, which seems remarkably true. What is he really like? people ask me. There are many different answers, but there is one theory— held by most Filipinos—that Manny Pacquiao, age thirty-one, the most significant boxer to come along since Ali, acts like a child because he had no childhood.

1

THE CITY OF DUST

MANNY PACQUIAO grew up in the Sarangani province on the Philippines' Mindanao Island, a place known for abject poverty, Islamic terrorists, and most recently the massacre of several dozen journalists. This is the area, near Kibawe, an hour or so drive outside of General Santos City, in the depths of a coconut tree jungle, where Pacquiao lived the first ten years of his existence and still visits frequently. It's a great place for a nice Saturday afternoon of *horse fighting*. Horse fighting is based on the concept of arousing male jealousy. To begin the contest, a mare is tied to a rope in the middle of a corral. Then two male horses are brought to her. They are tremendously excited and attack each other ferociously. While the horses battle, their coats lathering, barefooted men bet their family's rice money and drink semi-warm Gold Eagle Beer. The air smells of dust and horse manure. When I witnessed the bouts, dubbed "Friendly Horse Fighting," the Miley Cyrus song "Party in the USA" was being played over a loud speaker; the men mouthing the lyrics. Most of the crowd hangs on the fence, ducking as the bucking horses pelt them with rocks in their fighting fury.

The VIPs sit under a ripped tarp to (somewhat) shield them from the punishing equatorial sun. The corral's luxury box is favored by Victor "Tata" Yap, a local political figure and longtime friend of Manny Pacquiao's. "To know Manny Pacquiao, you must come here," he says. The Mayor, as everyone calls him, wears an $8,000 Rolex Oyster Perpetual (a gift from Pacquiao). He likes to quote Barack Obama's message of "hope and change."

Yap is trying to wrestle political control of the area from his own brother whom he has hasn't spoken to for several years. It is a deadly rivalry that Manny Pacquiao will be drawn into within a few weeks. Tata, Pacquiao's operative, spits on the ground. "We use people in this country," he says. "Especially the poor."

Along with Tata, there is his assistant—who makes sure his boss's beer glass is full at all times—the bookmaker, and a policeman toting an M-16 who is charged with keeping Yap alive and out of kidnappers' hands. The steeds kick each other, rear up, gnaw each others' flanks, and try and tear at each other's manes. When one horse just can't take it any-more—his own blood or exhaustion usually does one in—it surrenders by running away. When this happens, the crowd simultaneously laughs and groans. This is one of those rare contests in which the winner gets to mount a mare at the end of the match. The men pay off their bets (the Mayor moans; he lost big on the grey "Romantico") and then trudge up the dirt road to the cockfighting arena, which is a pathetic wood structure that sits on a craggy hillside, just past the snorting pig and hundreds of people, most of whom seem extremely hungry. It is Filipino tradition to show their generosity by providing visitors with their finest cooking and apologize for it. "You like? You like? I'm sorry, we were not ready for you." The Mayor, who has a mechanical engineering degree, sips his beer, his gold bracelet encrusted with diamonds spelling MANNY—another gift from the fighter—dangling on his wrist. To help these villagers and deliver his own brand of change and hope, he is greasing palms by buying beers and showing his common man appeal: He wears the national uniform of T-shirt and flip flops, and as a crowd gathers around him, he expertly puts the razor blade on the leg of a rooster, which will be vomiting blood within minutes. Pacquiao, like many Filipino men, loves cockfighting, and Pacquiao even owns one thousand fighting birds, many of them imported from Texas. (I hear buzz that the doctor who circumcised the world champion is around, but before I can be introduced, I am situated at a place of honor inside the arena, a few feet from the fighting birds, while men whisper a warning, "If they get near you, move. The blade will slice you.") Several members of the crowd wear Pacquiao T-shirts and giggle, "The PacMan is my idol." When Pacquiao comes around here, he is welcomed, but his fame and fortune have risk, and he carries a pistol and armed guards protect him. He employs his own security force of at least thirty people and has more than 100 M-16s at his house. He needs to be cautious because he is a kidnap risk, but no Islamic extremist would actually kill him, someone assures me, because "they are warriors, and he is a warrior." This particular part of the Sarangani province is not far from the massacre in the Maguindanao province, where in November 2009, gunmen massacred fifty-seven men and women, including thirty journalists. The victims were shot dead and buried in mass graves near the highway where they were stopped. The victims—mostly relatives or supporters of a political rival who ran for governor against Andal Ampatuan Sr.—were murdered and mutilated; one victim had sixteen bullet wounds in her groin area. Andal Ampatuan Jr., a former vice mayor and scion of the politically powerful clan, has been accused of leading more than one hundred local police and militiamen in the ambush. A total of 197 suspects were charged with multiple murder counts, including family patriarch Ampatuan Sr. and other members of the clan that has ruled the impoverished province for years. At the end of July 2010, sixty-four suspects had been arrested and the others remained at large. All those in custody who have been arraigned have denied the charges against them and the Philippine government dropped charges against Ampatuan Jr.'s brothers—Zaldy and Akmad Ampatuan. The massacre was the single deadliest event ever recorded by the Committee to Protect Journalists. President Macapagal Arroyo—a Pacquiao supporter—imposed martial law (the first time since the dictatorship of Ferdinand Marcos, which ended in 1986) as the police and the military investigated the crime. Dozens of suspects were arrested and property and house raids yielded more than fifteen hundred weapons that the government said were being used in a rebellion. In the intertwined Filipino social structure, the Ampatuan family is one that everyone, including Pacquiao, knows well.

THIS PROVINCE, the place where Emmanuel Dapidran Pacquiao was born on December 17, 1978, is the fourth poorest in the Philippines, where boys risk their lives to climb coconut trees (to make fifty centavo per coconut), play basketball on dirt courts, ride four to a motorcycle, get addicted to *shabu* (a combination of meth and caffeine), and live in the endless crap, with roosters, goats, stray dogs, and no running water. Those lucky locals who get to eat more than once a day use their hands to eat rice, chicken, and hard-boiled eggs served in coconut leaves. Yap puts it succinctly, "These are the poorest of the poor; they are happy only when they have sex." Women have 3.27 children in the contraceptive-ambivalent Philippines, but Yap says in the countryside it is probably averaging six children, which leads to serious bonding time in overcrowded bamboo shacks. Disease and poor water quality are responsible for more than six out of ten Filipino children in the elementary school system having tapeworms, as the latter compounds the problem of malnutrition. Pacquiao has lived this life for a third of his existence. Not unlike a lot of children in the province, Pacquiao quit school by age ten. His teachers will tell you he was a good student— a kid who looked after others, too. Life was not so easy at home, and a father figure was barely present. His mother has been quoted numerous times saying that Pacquiao's father, Rosalio, killed and then ate the family dog, and then abandoned his family. "Manny could hardly eat three times a day," says Yap, who knew him as a child. Forty-five percent of families in his province are classified as living in poverty, but Pacquiao was considered poor, even among the poor. "He would borrow a glass of rice from neighbors, and they would mix it with water to make a porridge, enough to go around for six children." Pacquiao doesn't like to talk publicly about it, but he tells his friends that skipping two, even three, meals a day was not uncommon. It was a good night when the seven-member family could share a can of sardines for dinner, sitting on the dirt floor of their straw hut. They grew mealy vegetables, but the crops were so inconsistent (no fertilizer was available) and meager that the family had difficulty surviving.

THE NIGHT BEFORE the horse fights, a friend and I drove through the jungle in a speeding van, whizzing past military checkpoints, and Abu Sayyaf and Moro Islamic Liberation Front strongholds to reach Pacquiao's security force before nightfall. There are countless private armies in the country, and so journalists and aid workers cross their fingers and jump from one secure caravan to the next, trying to negotiate between different factions. The American-built roads are well-paved and the better houses are made of cinderblocks. Fences are sticks stuck in mud, fish for sale hang from poles, people burn coconut shells for fuel. Children leave school late in the evening as there are not enough schools so they have to teach the kids in three-hour shifts. At one point along the highway, there is a sign shaped like a coffin, "Free Coffin Courtesy of Manny Pacquiao." My friend tells me that no one can afford to bury their dead in this province, so Pacquiao foots the bill. He donates hospital beds and hands out school supplies to poor students.

We eventually reach Pacquiao's abode as night falls. We emerge from the jungle to shake Pacquiao's hand as he strolls down a street, dozens of excited fans following him. He is amused but not surprised to see us. Pacquiao believes in the concept of fate. Everything, you see, is meant to be. Eventually, we have dinner at his house, in the town of Kiamba, and at 8 p.m. Pacquiao sits through a grueling political strategy meeting in which operatives plead for more of his quickly evaporating money. They talk until three in the morning. Pacquiao often goes for several nights without sleeping, and he has been known to simply pass out. So I started talking with "Tata" Yap, and he invited me to his house the next day. I had learned awhile ago that just showing up at someone's house, from peasant to president, will usually bring an invitation for conversation, food, and drink. I was amused, a week hence, when I read the *Manila Bulletin* and Pacquiao's adviser, Michael Koncz, a Canadian, was quoted saying that even if the enormously popular U.S. news program *60 Minutes* comes to the Philippines, Manny won't have time for it. Manny Pacquiao invites thousands of people to his own birthday party. For a Filipino, Koncz's inhospitable statement might have been realistic, but it went against their nature.

While Filipinos love Pacquiao, behind his back they make fun of his accent when he speaks English, the language of the educated class. It is like Rafael Nadal speaking English: It sort of makes sense, but it's challenging to decipher. Western reporters and photographers who try and get to know him are often ignored, and interview requests are agreed upon and then forgotten. Manny Pacquiao is a difficult man to pin down. There is a familiarity with Pacquiao in the Philippines that makes him a friend to his people. "Filipinos know he has been to hell and back; they understand him," says Chino Trinidad, the journalist. It is six degrees of Manny Pacquiao.

In the United States, there is a game called the "Six Degrees of Separation from Kevin Bacon" in which people figure out how they are related or have a connection to the movie actor. No one usually claims to *know* Kevin Bacon.

When Filipinos talk about Pacquiao, they are very familiar with everything about his story, but when pressed if they have actually met him, they usually look into their soup. To spend any time with him, one must develop connections, most of which are totally unreliable. The entourage text certain people up-to-the-minute itineraries: "Pacquiao napping." It's purposefully casual and unpredictable. The coterie of Filipino journalists who have covered him from the beginning are always the first to know everything. They are most accurately described as 1950s-era American journalists who run, play basketball, and even drink with Pacquiao. Pacquiao trusts them because they can't afford to hurt him. In the United States, journalists cover him, too, but boxing is not the sport it once was, so the reporters are not as relentless, constant, or as trustworthy. He tends to care about his own constituency and eyes American journalists with a great deal of suspicion. Earlier in 2009, a *GQ* magazine writer and photographer, naïve about the ways of Manny Pacquiao and his team, had flown to Manila to meet with him for a profile story. They waited and waited. They made frantic calls. And, of course, no one ever showed up. Never rely on people who "know" Pacquiao because millions upon millions of Filipinos will claim friendship with the man. The people surrounding him try and keep people at bay. He is surrounded by dozens upon dozens of lackeys who exist to satisfy his every whim—from fluffing his rice to testing the temperature of his drinking water. Only a few of his most exclusive facilitators get glimpses into his frailty and bad habits and are tasked with staying silent. The two Filipino television networks, which travel with him and broadcast nightly video updates of his whereabouts, are tolerated as long as they play the game nicely. (He has his own show on one of the networks.) In *Pacquiao: The Movie*, a highly fictionalized and—by Filipino standards—big budget movie of his life, journalists were depicted as gossipy nuisances, and yet in press conferences he lavishes reporters with praise, and Filipino writers constantly announce that he is the country's greatest national hero. But when I ask a personal question, he is likely to respond, "I let you be here, to see my life, what else do you want?" as if you are stealing his soul.

I showed up the following day at the Mayor's house, near the village of Pacquiao's youth. To get to Yap's residence, we drove past the Mayor's cock farm, armed guard, and security gate. Once we entered his modest compound, dozens of people, including his security detail, were lounging around outside. The mayor sat at a desk while people, many of whom looked sickly or beaten down by exhaustion and the tropical heat wave, presented him with doctor's bills. He looked over the crumpled papers and did his best not to look outwardly exasperated. I asked him what he was doing, and he told me that he, or more accurately, Manny Pacquiao, was paying the bills out of his own pocket. If sick and in need of care, the villagers travel, usually by motorcycle, to a clinic in General Santos City. They return with hospital invoices and bills for prescriptions that they can't possibly pay. For working 3 a.m. to 9 p.m. at a local coconut plantation, a man

makes two dollars. One elderly gentleman, looking morti-
fied, had walked barefoot for nearly a day in the hope that
Pacquiao would shell out fifty dollars for his family's medical
expenses. "Is this a good way to run a country, to have the
poor beg and Manny Pacquiao to pay their medical bills?"
the Mayor asks. To help eliminate this sort of begging and
inefficiency, Pacquiao wants to build a hospital in the area.
He felt unChristianlike to brag, but I found out that he is the
area's welfare system, as well as paying for various things,
such as athletic fees (MP Karate Studio Scholarship Fund),
arts programs (Manny Pacquiao dance troupe), and countless other social programs. A local kid had lost her leg, and
Pacquiao had paid for the operation, rehabilitation expenses,
and a prosthetic. The procedure and fake leg would have
financially ruined her family. Pacquiao's ultimate pride
comes from paying for impoverished children to go to school
as "Pacquiao scholars," of which there are more than five
hundred. Twenty-one years ago, the PacMan had not been
able to stay in school, as his family left the jungle and tried
its luck in the nearest metropolis.

PEOPLE WHO can't make it in Mindanao's rural
provinces often end up migrating to General Santos City, a
hard-scrabble coastal city that reeks of fish. It's about an
hour away from Pacquiao's birthplace, if one speeds through
and ignores all the military checkpoints. It has a population
of more than five hundred thousand with a $50 million air-
port that was funded by the United States and built in 1996.
There is decent—yet chaotically planned—road infrastruc-
ture, built with American aid, to help get fish and plantation

fruit to faraway lands, and there is a rundown mall (the site of an Islamic terrorist bombing a few years ago where several children were killed). But it's mostly shacks and a frantic cavalcade of 100cc motorcycles and tricycle cabs. For years, people called it the "City of Dust," but city leaders prefer "Tuna Capital of the Philippines." General Santos City faces Sarangani Bay, which has access to Moro Gulf and the Celebes Sea, a rich source of commercial fishing. The city's economic engine comes from its large seaport, where more than fifty vessels bring in yellow fin tuna, tilapia, and other creatures that are processed in the five canning plants, taken to the country's populace, to Manila, and beyond. (Sashimi grade goes directly to Japanese sushi distributors.) Piles and piles of dead sea life are brought to the enormous local fish market, which is thriving with pickpockets and aggressive teenage beggars, and then on to the GenSan's tuna shacks that seem to be on every street corner. The local delicacies are *tuna kinilaw*—a delicious ceviche with pepper, cucumber, lime, lemon, and raw tuna—which is dipped in a sauce made from soy, lime, and peppers. And grilled tuna shoulder (*tuna belly ihaw*). The smell of grilled fish mixes with raw sewage. Stray dogs, roosters, and the occasional pig and oxen roam the streets.

The Pacquiaos of General Santos City were not a rich family. They ended up living near a river where people bathe, wash clothes, and hope to escape with their lives during flood season. There were six children—Liza, Domingo, Isidra, Manny, Bobby, Rogelio—at the Pacquiao hovel. His mother, Dionisia, ended up as a washerwoman and sold rice cakes on the streets. Many of the residents are poor tuna fishermen,

yet growing up, Pacquiao and his family were so impoverished that their neighbors pitied them. "He was a bright boy
but didn't finish school because of poverty," says a childhood
acquaintance. "You could tell how poor his family was by
his clothes." Manny, the dropout, swept up and racked balls
at billiards shacks for tips, as well as sold cigarettes and *pan
de sal* on the streets. He was known to give his unsold bread
to poor children. Like many people in the Philippines, the
Pacquiaos practiced a medieval type of Catholicism. They
were especially devout and mystical in their belief. The
Philippines, the twelfth most populated country in the world,
is the one nation in which Catholicism is actually growing.
When Pacquiao gets hit with a good shot in the ring he will
sometimes laugh, as a reminder of his own weakness under
God. In every speech I have ever heard him give, he profusely
thanks God.

Left by two husbands, his mother woke her children at
dawn so they could pray together. "Manny has a strong mind
and a strong body," says his mother, who shares her son's
athletic frame. "Just like his mother. Except I am stronger."
She is a charismatic figure and now has her own weekly television program called "The PacMom," and more than a few
Filipinos, from shoeshine boys to governors, have told me
that they are fans of her work as an actor because she is
"very natural," particularly in a recent movie in which she
co-starred with the country's ex-president.

While Catholicism preaches a national humility, the way
Filipinos perceive themselves also comes from their underdog role in Southeast Asia where every country has seen significant economic improvements in the last two decades,

except their archipelago of 7,107 islands. Taken over by the Spanish, Americans, and the Japanese, ruled by clans, and given to blind obedience to the Church, the Philippines has never experienced an economic revolution. The Philippines is built on a cruel disparity, in which the most talented of the lower class move to other countries. While they send back money to their families, they create a lasting dependence in the homeland. Imelda Marcos, the wife of one of the most notorious dictators in modern history, is still active in politics; she is the patron saint of the rich, and even the people who endured her husband's rule seem to forgive his atrocities. ("Filipinos are forgiving and crazy," a newspaper columnist who was once fired from his job for supporting Corey Aquino told me. "Manny Pacquiao is no different.") Thirty-three percent of the population lives below the poverty line, and forty-four percent of Filipinos subsist on US$2 or less a day. The southern Philippines' island of Mindanao is one of the country's most violent and poor. And this makes Pacquiao's life story even more profound to his countrymen. People ridicule him for a lack of intelligence because his spoken English is practically unintelligible—he understands it perfectly—and to some listeners his use of language is unrefined; for womanizing ("I have one wife, and five girlfriends . . . just like Pacquiao" goes the joke), and the sketchy people around him (war and gambling lords). They can joke about him, but they also can't help but admire him. He astonishes them. And being in his presence washes their sins away. *Do you know what he came from?* The richest and the poorest say it. Well. Do. You? This is the reality, not the mythos of Pacquiao. Filipinos see him, at the height of his career and worldwide celebrity, as a demigod who emerged from the City of Dust.

At the beginning, Manny Pacquiao was just another GenSan urchin. At age twelve, he saw some adults, including his uncle, huddle around a television set. They were watching Mike Tyson lose to underdog Buster Douglas (a 42–1 underdog) in Tokyo. Pacquiao had always been enthralled with boxing, but Tyson's loss seemed to inspire Pacquiao even more. He started attending the fights in downtown GenSan. Pacquiao's wayward father, who would see him on occasion, remembers his son putting gravel into a rice sack, taking off his T-shirt to make gloves, and striking the handmade heavy bag. "He was always practicing boxing from the age of ten until now," says his father. "He was a very good kid. No golden spoon." (Despite his father leaving his mother, Manny has given his fifty-two-year-old progenitor—a chain-smoker who now sports a Lacoste gold bracelet—a house, its pink color standing out on a rural road where kids piss in the trenches and stray dogs run wild.)

His mother watched him pretend to be a professional boxer, too. His speedbag was a pair of old flip-flops hanging from a tree.

There was also something serious about Pacquiao at an early age that made him want to take care of those around him. His mother thought he should be a priest. But Pacquiao, who likes to say "I'm a nice guy," did not shy away when friends got into neighborhood free-for-alls, or *bukbukan*— unrestrained fistfighting. If another street kid selling bread or doughnuts encroached on his turf, he would fight to defend it. "When I was young, that's all I wanted to do, fight, fight,

fight," he says. In a variety of street fights, he proved emi-
nently successful. Pierce Egan, the first notable chronicler of
the sweet science, wrote, in *Boxiana*, "It is winning the purse
that gains the boxer friends—it procures him fame; he
acquires notoriety—and, if he does not make a fortune, he
obtains a handsome living. It also enables the pugilist to mix
with superior society—it enlarges his mind—and, according
to his deserts, so he is respected; all of which tend to make
him a better man." Fighting could be Pacquiao's way out of
the gutter. Pacquiao was obsessed with boxing. By age thirteen, he had used his own hand to make a small boxing glove
tattoo on his chest.

In between selling goods on the street, the young
Pacquiao ventured down near the GenSan plaza to formally
run and train. Abner Cordero, a highly touted fighter,
worked out in a nearby gym with his father, Dizon Cordero.
Pacquiao had a youthful confidence and thought he could
become better than Cordero, the city's favorite boxing son,
and asked Dizon to train him. They ran on the oval track,
which had enough stray rocks and jagged unevenness to turn
the strongest ankle. Pacquiao ran on it in his bare feet.

On Sundays, the plaza would become a boxing arena for
amateur fights. One of Pacquiao's first trainers was Rudolpo
"Mukong" Nacionales, who still works in the area. When I
visited the place, roosters were scampering around as his
wife, Adeulisa, who used to click the stopwatch for
Pacquiao's training runs ("He was very fast"), said the children in the stable fight for 250 pesos (US$5) per bout. If they
win, they get to buy rice, and everyone can eat. "No prize, no
eat," she told me. To make enough to sustain themselves, the

young boxers sell cigarettes out of a clear plastic box. They train on a concrete slab, hitting an inner tube filled with dirt. Like most boxing gyms in the Philippines, there are bunk beds so the fighters have a place to sleep.

Seventeen-year-old amateur boxer Joel D. Bieton (45–5) works out with Nacionales. He is fatherless and dreams of fame and fortune. He told me, "I would like to be like Manny. Praise of God. Only God can make that." It was pretty much the same life for Pacquiao. He also sold cigarettes, and he fought for a measly one hundred pesos [less than three dollars]. To regulars of the Sunday plaza fights, he was always very courageous and had natural speed and developing power, but he wasn't considered a clever boxer. Kids would go into the jungle, go to the ring, which was often just a cleared dirt patch, kick off their flip-flops and T-shirts and put on shared gloves. The children were a rural amusement, like horses fighting or roosters slicing each other with a razor blade taped to their wrinkled legs. Pacquiao would pursue his opponent like a crazed dog. He was a frantic, inaccurate puncher, his gloves active but flailing. The crowd loved him. They talked about him. Pleasing the people became as important to him as winning. The malnourished ninety-pound-nothing knew how to win by overwhelming his opponents with speed and risk. He fought more than thirty times without a loss. He couldn't fight enough. "His courage is such that his fights are half over before they begin," says Rudy Salud, a longtime associate. "His courage comes from poverty, from having lived that way." Pacquiao agrees. Without his background on the mean streets of Mindanao, he says, "I never would have been a champion."

He also couldn't have made it without his boxing buddies. They were a good group and they watched each others' backs. The GenSan kids had talent, but they were moving in place. They trained, they fought, they won. And they starved. A local talent scout told them that to make their dreams come true they had to go to the big city. Abner Cordero, Pacquiao, and Eugene Barutag were the greatest prospects. They needed to get away from Sarangani province.

The bright lights (when there isn't a brownout) of Manila beckoned him. Manila has a mystical allure to rural Filipinos who watch soap operas about the city's rich and fantasize about making their own fortune there. Jose Rizal, the Philippines' first major patriot and martyr, called it a "world of parasites, bores, and hangers-on, whom God in His infinite bounty creates and so kindly multiplies in Manila." But Filipinos are used to moving for economic salvation. While Filipinos base their lives on family, familial proximity is constantly broken as children and adults chase faraway jobs. Thirteen percent of its gross domestic product comes from remittance, and its banking system is built around the billions made in wire service fees. (Even in remote areas, the most bedraggled people discover that I am from California, approach me, and tell me they have a relative in Los Angeles; U.S. work visas are a precious commodity because the dollars sent home can support a family of eight.) Pacquiao admits that at age fifteen, he had a difficult time breaking away from his mother. He told her obliquely, "Don't worry, Mommy, I will get us out of this," and he made his own runaway plans.

Without enough money for an $80 plane ticket, he decided to travel by boat, but he didn't even have the $50 for sea travel. But his impoverished pals, who had already moved to Manila, including Robert Varron, Eugene Barutag, and six others, were able to pool their money and buy Pacquiao a ticket. He then went down to the General Santos port, past the rifle-carrying guards and the white-booted fish butchers, and sailed away on a Manila-bound ferry.

2

THE STREETS OF MANILA

MANNY PACQUIAO walks into a ridiculously frilly banquet room in Manila's Sofitel Philippine Plaza on March 25, 2010. Despite the stifling heat outside, Pacquiao is dressed in a bespoke dark suit. He has barely removed his tie since arriving in Manila several days earlier. The Banquet of Champions will be televised, and since Pacquiao is running for Congress, he wants to appear as a serious young man. A visual and musical cacophony of blinking lights and pounding techno music, along with the rather silly sight of boxers and trainers dressed in formal wear, greets him with an explosive ovation. Instead of his usual let's-have-a-laugh expression, his jaw is tightened. It throws people off. *Who is this guy?* He takes his chair next to Laura Elorde, the widow of Gabriel "Flash" Elorde, the Philippines' last great sports icon. "Mama"—with sprightly grey hair—is the grand dame of Filipino boxing, and when people greet her, they bow their heads and kiss her hand in respect, as though she were a queen.

A couple days after the banquet, I visited Elorde in her home, a swinging sixties pad gone to seed. It is in what was once the outskirts of Manila. Her husband's black Ford

Mustang, with a tarp over it, sits in the living room. She has a dusty trophy room showing off Flash's title belts, shorts, gloves, and shoes. She's lucky to still have it all. After the place was repossessed by the banks, President Ferdinand Marcos—a boxing fanatic—issued a special decree to give it back to the Elorde family. A two-minute walk from her residence is the Elorde Sports Center, a three-thousand-seat cockfighting arena. A stray rooster or two wander around. Men from Manila used to bring their kids to meet Flash—a sports hero in a land that produces one every twenty, thirty, sometimes fifty years—and the children would shake the man's hand and then go outside and play in the countryside while the men bragged about past glory. Up until the early 1980s, this area was threaded with rice fields. But now Manila's sprawl has overtaken this formerly bucolic section, which is teeming with traffic and crime.

Flash, who held the junior lightweight title for seven years during the sixties, has gone, too. He is "waiting for us," as the Filipinos say. Flash was a chain smoker who would try to smoke at least one cigarette between rounds. He died of lung cancer in 1985 at age forty-nine. Mama has anointed Pacquiao the new Flash, and she thinks of Manny as one of her own sons. "Manny makes mistakes, he is young, and he is misguided—because of the people around him—but he is *the best*. He is so humble. . . . Did you see what he did the other night?"

At the banquet, Pacquiao accepted the "Fighter of the Decade" award, gave a wistful speech ("What we do in life lasts an eternity . . . everyone has a calling . . ."), signed autographs until three in the morning, and capped the night off when the performer Justin Timberlake, in town for a concert, asked him to pose for a photograph. But that was not what made Mama Elorde so proud. Z Gorres, a bantam-weight, was also at the party. He had won a bout in Las Vegas in November 2009, but after the win, Gorres collapsed in the ring because of a brain hemorrhage and went into a coma. He was now recovering back in the Philippines. He sat, sort of out of it, at a table at the Banquet of Champions. Pacquiao looked him in his cloudy eyes and quietly slipped him a check for one million pesos, or $22,000, a tremendous sum in the Philippines. Pacquiao whispered to him that he wanted Gorres to use the money to start a new life. In the minds of Filipinos, Pacquiao's virtues of kindness and humility trump his boyish transgressions. This is the concept of *Hiya*, a Tagalog term meaning "face." Showing due respect to elders and acting kindly toward family and strangers are all ways to gain face and remain a part of the Filipino tribe. As one grows richer, the commitments become mind-boggling because you become a highly sought-after godparent, which creates a network of ritual relatives, sometime numbering five hundred or more. Because everyone seems to let them down, Filipinos primarily rely on each other. The bond of family, a term loosely defined, is unshakeable.

Pacquiao might have a house in Manila's exclusive Laguna neighborhood, near where his children go to private school, but as someone told me, "He is like us; he is with us."

IT HAD BEEN sixteen years since Pacquiao was a stowaway bound for Manila, the decaying capital of the Philippines. It's one of Southeast Asia's most impoverished capital cities, a modern Third World metropolis created by the worst of colonial intentions and a parade of some of the most ridiculous dictators ever to walk the earth. Even Manila's well-off cannot totally escape the city that they have helped create: A trip to a shopping mall, restaurant, or five-star hotel involves machine gun–carrying guards and a canine unit that checks vehicles for bombs or guns. Even the most exclusive areas, such as Metro Manila's Makati City, are within fifty feet of endless shantytowns, which catch fire on a regular basis. One in five children must forego school for work and walk through the busiest of traffic without a care for life or limb. Impoverished men who cannot find work drown their days with a mixture of Colt 45 beer and homemade gin. A typhoon in 2009 submerged 80 percent of the city in mud, and the city's bayside dump, with its black clouds of flies, has four thousand residents. One of Manila's inexplicable tourist attractions is the Hobbit House, a bar in which the waiters are all dwarfs.

Manny Pacquiao, a sticklike fifteen-year-old stowaway, and his GenSan boxing buddies, arrived in this hellhole to make a name for themselves. They didn't have any money or the promise of a job, but they made a pact to help each other and not beg. The GenSan boys slept in cramped rooms together, a common practice among the indentured populace. They ended up in Malabon, where they became boxers of Polding Correa, Pacquiao's first manager. They slept next to each other on the floor. One of their roommates, Eddie Cadalzo, a young amateur, who slept in Pacquiao's quarters, died in his sleep one evening. No one is sure why.

Despite his current fame and fortune, Pacquiao continues to have people sleep on the floor next to him. So when American television host Jimmy Kimmel would ask him, years later, about his entourage and wonder why they slept around his bed, Pacquiao looked desperately confused. He was unable to *really* explain it.

The GenSan boys sold doughnuts and worked construction (once he didn't eat for four days because his employer didn't pay him). If one member of the group had money, rice was purchased for the group. Manny was so good-hearted that he would often forgo his share so someone else could have more. When other boxers would leave the gym as a group to get a bite, Pacquiao would hang back, never wanting to be a charity case. In a letter to his mother, he told her not to worry: "Life is difficult here. There are times when I eat rice only once a day." ("I wept when I read it," she says.) Since they were underaged, employers took advantage of them and stole or simply didn't bother to pay them their wages. And there were difficulties. Some of his friends developed an addiction to the crack pipe. "Manny would drink, and drink a lot, and he also smoked," Vice Governor Emmanuel Pinol told me. Pinol, who has fallen out of friendship with Pacquiao, knew him in the early days. "There is a dark side to Manny." Among the boxers, there were many incidents of hepatitis, common among drug users and boxers who have sustained liver damage. There were bar fights and fatal stabbings. Two of Manny's best friends died within a year.

As directed by his General Santos boxing connections, Pacquiao found his way to the L&M Gym in the Quiapo area of Manila. Financiers and housing developers have allowed this historic and architecturally rich part of Manila the chance to rot. There are abandoned administration buildings (inspired by the American architect Daniel Burnham, who designed much of the architecture of Washington, DC), unused train stations, and thick-walled churches in the Spanish style, some painted in bright colors. ("I used to work in that building," someone told me, in a deadpan voice. "It was condemned after an earthquake, but someone put a coat of paint on it. Now it is fine.") Between the wide, European-inspired avenues, some graced with palm trees, are alleys filled with prototypically mildewy Southeast Asian apartments, which might not endure typhoon season. There are meat and flower markets. Workers move in and out of basements filled with goods and cart them to storefronts, splashing pushcarts through tepid water.

The L&M stood (it was torn down in early 2009) a few buildings onto Paquita Street. Established in 1978, it was a well-known place in Filipino boxing circles. Boxing writers spent their days watching pros train at the L&M, let their own children go at the heavy bag, and interviewed the prospects who would stand in the alley. In the fate-obsessed Philippines, it was known as a lucky gym for producing champions, but it was considered (with a sick sense of pride) the planet's worst-smelling boxing establishment. (Chino Trinidad, the Filipino boxing commentator, who spent a lot of time in the place, says he still can't get the unusual stench out of his nose.) An open toilet, similar to one found in a prison cell, was in one corner. There was no smoking allowed inside the gym, probably due to the tar paper walls, but butts would somehow get on the canvas, and the boxers would sleep on them to cushion their frames. Besides the human waste and discarded cancer sticks, the fighters "swam in their own sweat" in the low-ceilinged gym. Most boxing gyms are hot, but the L&M, which was open twenty-four hours a day, was so oppressive that trainers compared it to sparring in a sauna—eight rounds at the L&M was like going for twelve in a regular joint. "You couldn't breathe," one regular told me. Subsequent to training at the L&M, boxers, including Pacquiao, had difficulty finding as "authentic" a place to train for their fights. Manny's brother, Bobby, 30, also a professional boxer, once tried to train at a brand-new facility but could barely get through his session because it didn't "smell right."

"When Pacquiao came here, he didn't have anything," says Ramon "Moy" Lainez, the "L" in the L&M. "He was a stowaway, and he wasn't very strong. We didn't expect much from him. He had a big heart, he really wanted to fight, he really trained, and he dreamed that someday he will be a world champion." Pacquiao tended to train on his own, but he was required to pay one of the trainers one peso per day. He worked constantly on fundamentals: his stance and balance. One of the credos in the L&M was if you had no balance, you couldn't throw hard punches. Lainez would watch Pacquiao—who he knew was missing meals—work diligently on his developing footwork ("It was inborn"), but his punching was so unrefined ("It was like he was swimming") and his body so malnourished ("Skinnnnnn-eee, and not very strong") that he didn't think much of his boxing future, except for his superhuman capacity for hard work and his toe-to-toe courage. Lainez was even more surprised when

Pacquiao talked of winning world championships and how he would use his fame. "He told me he wanted to be a politician and help the poor. 'This is my dream,' he would say, 'This is my dream.'"

Pacquiao fought in run-for-cover, barely legal smokers, pulled together in Manila's cramped suburbs. Boxing writers saw him wrap his own hands, real tight, and go through his frantic training and laughed at his over exuberance. No one had to push him to train hard, and Pacquiao had the ability to ignore his hunger pangs better than any of the young fighters at the gym. The beat writers would buy him bread sometimes and give him coffee filled to the brim with sugar. They knew he couldn't pay them back so they tried to do it anonymously, buying food as a communal practice so no one lost face.

ONE MORNING Ronnie Nathanielsz invited me to his modest Manila apartment for breakfast (rice, noodles, beef, instant coffee). Originally from Sri Lanka, Nathanielsz talks with a distinct colonial English accent. In the 1960s, he was the radio voice of Flash Elorde's fights. He worked as Ferdinand Marcos's liaison officer to Muhammad Ali for the Thrilla in Manila. Nathanielsz, who is very genial, made sure the dictator could watch any and every boxing broadcast in the Malacanang, the ornate presidential palace. He has a great admiration for boxers, particularly Pacquiao. "If Pacquiao was an arrogant sonofabitch, no one would pay him any attention," he says. "The frenzy around Pacquiao is worse than around Ali. With Ali they were in awe, with Pacquiao the people are fanatical."

Nathanielsz, funny, profane and articulate, makes no apologies for his support of Marcos, the country's notorious dictator. But many people cannot forget his interview with Marcos's foe and the country's martyr, Benigno Aquino Jr. In 1978 (the year in which Pacquiao was born), Aquino—Marcos's charismatic opponent—was in prison, mostly held in solitary confinement. Marcos had rung him up on trumped-up charges. From his cell, Aquino led the People's Power movement and ran for president despite being incarcerated. Under enormous pressure to show the world that he was running a fair election (even though many thought it was fixed), Marcos allowed Aquino to appear on *Face the Nation*, hosted by Nathanielsz. Despite enduring a forty-day hunger strike and time in solitary confinement, Aquino showed an embarrassing level of wit and intelligence. To this day, people might snicker about Nathanielsz—*"marcos boy yan"*—but an equal number of Filipinos adore the Marcos name. Many pundits believe Marcos's son, Ferdinand Jr., known as Bongbong, who is currently a senator, will become president within the decade. Imelda might be a worldwide punch line but she continues to generate popular support at home. Nathanielsz has been an influential broadcaster throughout his entire career, and he would eventually become the voice of Pacquiao. In the mid-1990s, Nathanielsz was approached by Rod Nazario who was managing and housing several fighters, including Manny Pacquiao. Nazario and Nathanielsz had gone back a ways in the Philippines' small boxing community. While a bit player by American standards, Nazario had extensive fight and media connections in Metro Manila. He was also a decent idea man. He brought a modest proposal to

Nathanielsz—a boxing show that would televise professional fights around the city. Looking for more sports programming on his station, Nathanielsz jumped at the idea. He quickly bootstrapped a program, *Blow by Blow*. Nathanielsz, who many Filipinos—politics aside—consider the voice of boxing, would be the lead broadcaster.

Within the filthy confines of the L&M, the prospect of fighting on television got everyone stoked. Pacquiao was desperate to get in on the action, but he looked like he was a couple years from shaving. He was only sixteen, and a professional fighter had to be eighteen, so he simply lied about his age. It was his friend Eddie Varron, from General Santos City, who helped him fake the license administered by the Games and Amusements Board. (When Pacquiao later renewed his license, Varron was suspended for six months.) At weigh-ins, Pacquiao was so slight that a couple people told me he put heavy objects into his underwear to reach the minimum weight requirements. While he was training for his first pro fight, he tried gaining more weight. He had a torturously dull and dangerous job at a factory scraping rust out of the recycled metals, which paid him 160 pesos a day (or $3.55). "Now I can eat three times a day," he told his mother in a letter. "He said he missed me. . . . He was very young. . . . And that I could call him once a week," she said.

His professional debut was a scheduled four-rounder against Edmund Enting Ignacio, on January 22, 1995, which Pacquiao won on points.

It happened in round two. Manny Pacquiao wearing white shorts, trimmed in red, on television for the first time: July 1,

1995. He started throwing haymakers with both hands. Dele Decierto, clad in red, returned fire. And so it went for almost the entire round. Pacquiao's head was sloped down, like he was looking for a lost coin, but he continued to move forward and strike Decierto's torso. He used his right hand to jab, and then threw left hooks. While Pacquiao tended to hit and then keep his right hand down, Decierto couldn't counter Pacquiao's darting speed. But it was Pacquiao's power that would stop Decierto. Barely more than 110 pounds, Pacquiao pivoted his hips so well (visible only in slow motion) that his punches were devastatingly powerful. Decierto turned his back on Pacquiao with nineteen seconds left in the round. He was toast. The accumulation of body shots had been too much.

PACQUIAO FELL ILL a few days after his debut as the Filipino boxer showed manifestations of hepatitis when his eyes and skin turned yellowish, prompting him to seek medical attention. Pacquiao recovered enough to fight again, and then he told his mother to watch television the following Saturday. His mother didn't have a TV, so she went to a downtown appliance store in the City of Dust. Her son took on Rocky Palma. Pacquiao outpointed him in six rounds. He was now 2–0 as a professional.

To most observers, Pacquiao seemed like one of the millions of bedraggled and underfed Manila street kids, burnt by the sun. Pacquiao would show up early for his televised bouts to play pickup basketball with the television crew. The cameramen and commentators had no idea who the hell he was. About his first encounter with Pacquiao, a *Blow by*

Blow staffer told me, "I thought he was a homeless kid; I felt sorry for him." And then they saw Pacquiao fight. "He hadn't a clue, but he had courage," says Nathanielsz. "He threw punches, like my god, from all angles. Totally out of control. But incredible courage. That was the only thing. I could never have guessed what he would be today. This country was down in the pits. No respect. No recognition. No nothing. He gave it back to us. Through his fists. And through his charisma."

MANY OF THE *Blow by Blow* fights were held in Mandaluyong, a barangay of east Manila, in an open-air gymnasium next to a police station. When I went there one day, the constant noise of Manila traffic was inescapable. The gym's caretaker led me to a place under the stands. Like everyone in the bedeviled country, he wanted to reveal Pacquiao to me. He smiled and nodded his head over and over and pointed at a dank space. There was the chatter of children and the smells of cooking food. It was a cage where Pacquiao slept under the stands before his fights. It was another tortured cell from which Pacquiao had ascended. The gymnasium resembles an American middle school gym with stands filled with rows of chipped yellow plastic chairs. For fighting in the four-rounders, Pacquiao was given eight hundred pesos, or forty dollars. Of that, he spotted his trainer 15 percent, and if he was cut and someone had to sew him up, well, the eight hundred pesos wouldn't even be enough for his tetanus shot. As his reputation as a knockout artist grew, the people—in their flip-flops and sleeveless shirts—would come in droves. He was still a part of them then. Close enough to touch. He quickly rose from four-rounders, to eight-rounders, to scheduled ten-rounders and *Blow by Blow* began focusing its coverage around his performances, but his managers were having difficulty finding anyone who would even fight him.

A bout on October 21, 1995, was a typical Pacquiao affair. Pacquiao (7–0, 2 KOs) went against Renato Mendones in Puerto Princesa, about three hundred miles from Manila. Pacquiao was an ancient seventeen now but still looked years younger. He had a tendency to let his opponents punch him, then he paused a beat and unleashed a blinding volley. Pacquiao, a southpaw, smashed Mendones with a punishing straight left in the second round. Mendones looked like he wanted to *will* Pacquiao away from him, but he couldn't escape. "Mendones is getting a bad beating! *A bad beating!*" Pacquiao hit him with rights and lefts, and Mendones wobbled around the ring. "He's a bloody mess! Pacquiao is looking for the *coup de grâce*. It's over! *What a fighter!* Manny Pacquiao remains unbeaten. He has survived the first test of his professional career!" And so it went, month after month.

Pacquiao was fighting every six weeks, which kept him in fighting shape and also helped him better learn his craft. (Sugar Ray Robinson, considered the best boxer ever, used to fight every three weeks.) Sponsors started asking about Pacquiao. Pacquiao didn't crush his opponents with any apparent psychological gamesmanship, cruel relish, or visible anger. He took on some tough and desperate men who would do anything to win—intentionally step on his feet or elbow him out of the clinch or hit him low or butt the crap out of his skull. They wanted to eat and feed their families, too.

Pacquiao refused to foul his opponent or disrespect a referee. The commentators started noting it, creating this image of pure sportsmanship around him. With Pacquiao, Filipinos brag tirelessly about his sportsmanship. They wear T-shirts that read "One Man Practicing Sportsmanship Is Better Than 100 People Teaching It." Outside the ring and away from his TV appearances, though, he was developing some unholy habits—downing multiple San Miguel Light beers and "dating" numerous women. Pacquiao admits he drank and gambled in those days, after he temporarily abandoned the devout Catholic faith he was raised in. "I lost that for a while when I came to Manila," Pacquiao says. "But God was always looking out for me." He started having difficulty making weight, and he was getting cocky after eleven straight wins. Nathanielsz could see it in his eyes, and he told someone, "One day this guy is going to get knocked out."

Boxers don't like to wear long hair because it impairs their vision as the sweat tends to clog their eyes. But Manny Pacquiao let his hair grow long anyway. It was a sign of youthful hubris. On January 13, 1996—Pacquiao was now legitimately eighteen, even though he already fought ten professional bouts—he was fighting in the San Miguel Main Event against Lito Torrejos of Cebu City. Pacquiao danced and lunged with his left. Torrejos counterpunched, and Pacquiao ducked and dove. Pacquiao looked the same, fight after fight. He refused to have a regular trainer. He wasn't learning any new moves. Why would he? In the fifth round, Torrejos got a serious cut, and the fight was stopped. Pacquiao was declared the winner. But Pacquiao was simply using his speed. A veteran boxer could figure out how to counter his pirouette/lunging straight left/jab/jab/piroutte/ lunging straight jab. He stood straight up and predictably backed away after throwing combos.

PACQUIAO WAS making enough money to eat. After a payday, he could take a car to the beach and guzzle beer, too. "He drank like a fish," someone told me. After a hard night out, the rest of the fighters would struggle to get out of bed for roadwork, but Manny would already be up and running at Razel Park, sweating away his sins. But a growth spurt and some hard living were making it tougher for him to make weight. On one February evening in 1996 he faced Rustico Torrecampo at the Mandaluyong Sports Complex. Torrecampo was a gym hand. His primary job was to put up the ring, and he boxed a little on the side. The matchmakers couldn't find anyone willing to fight Manny, who had annihilated eleven straight opponents, so they dug up Torrecampo. The guy had already been hired to dismantle the ring after his fight. But Torrecampo had a plan going into the contest. "I knew after throwing a jab he would follow up with a straight or an uppercut," said Torrecampo. "I waited for him to jab, then I countered." Pacquiao dominated Torrecampo for the first three rounds, but then Torrecampo seized on his chance. He caught Pacquiao with a right. Crumpled on the canvas, the ref in white shirt and black bow tie, cradled Pacquiao: "Pacquiao's eyes are crossed! His eyes are crossed!" Lights out. Then the television crew carried Pacquiao out of the ring (a clear violation of accepted medical practice). Pacquiao was blabbering, "What happened? What happened?" *You just* *lost the fight.* He didn't know what had hit him. It took him thirty minutes to realize that he lost his first professional bout . . . to a gym hand. After that, he knew that if he was going to make it big he had to discipline himself. It was a theme that would repeat itself years later.

After his loss, he went to Nazario, "Get me the best ten-rounder in this weight class." As for Torrecampo, he went on to bust his left wrist during a bout against Ricky Sales. He decided to forgo a visit to a doctor, retiring in 1997 with a record of 14–8–5, with 7 KOs. He still has a small bone sticking out of his left wrist, the result of the fracture not healing properly. After hanging up his gloves, Torrecampo worked six days a week, ten hours a day, loading furnaces at the Cathay Metal factory. His daily pay was 304 pesos, or $6.52. In 2006, he quit the job and set up a roving sidewalk business, selling *mami*—fried rice and beef "asado" in a bicycle cart. Torrecampo was allowed to park his sidecar near a health center in exchange for sweeping the streets in the vicinity. Then a man drove a garbage truck into his sidecar, spilling the food onto the street. Torrecampo demanded money for the damages. The man ignored him and drove away. Torrecampo ran after the truck, caught up with the man, jumped in the driver's seat, and allegedly stabbed him twice with a kitchen knife. Torrecampo, a father of three, who lived in a squatter's home, is wanted for murder and on the run.

PACQUIAO'S FAME was growing, but the prize-fighting money was so miniscule that Pacquiao was still living and training with his Mindanao friends, including the boxers

Bernie Torres and Eugene Barutag. His buddy Abner Cordero eventually became the Philippine bantamweight champion but retired prematurely after contracting hepatitis. One night, around Christmas of 1996, Pacquiao and Barutag were on the same fight card, which would unfold on a dreary basketball court in Sampaloc, considered a *depressed* area of Manila, which is saying something. Barutag and Pacquiao were best friends: They had learned how to survive on the mean Manila streets, and they vowed to support each other when one of them made it big. Barutag, a featherweight, was going up against Randy Andaga, a journeyman, on the undercard. Barutag dominated the early rounds and almost knocked out his opponent. Most ringside observers thought the fight should have been halted, but Andagan got his second wind and the eight-rounder became a blind slugfest. At the end of the fight, Barutag collapsed. Since there was no physician or medical team present, some people lugged Barutag into a television vehicle and Chino Trinidad—now a well-known Filipino sports commentator—frantically drove the vehicle to Jose Reyes Hospital. Barutag was barely breathing and put on a respirator. The physician injected him with adrenaline. Trinidad was the only person there for him. "The doctor asked me, 'Who are his closest relatives?' I said, 'Honestly, I don't know. They are just fighters and we are just TV coverers. We don't know where his parents are. We don't know where his closest of kin are.' The doctor told me that Barutag had expired." Since Manny was fighting in the main event, the organizers elected not to tell him until after his bout. Pacquiao had seen Barutag leave the gym unconscious and was visibly worried. Pacquiao was 18. After his victory, they broke the news to him. Pacquiao took it upon himself to pay for the funeral (the family couldn't afford it) and refused to leave the open casket for three nights.

"You talk of tragedy, you talk of heartbreak, and Manny has had it," says Trinidad. "All his life, the sad story that has befallen him would probably . . . you put it on someone else, and a guy would probably commit suicide. Manny is someone who keeps his emotions to himself. He doesn't show the world that he is hurt. He has this ability to keep the pain to himself, which, to this day, helps him."

Pacquiao took on some stiffs and crumpled them to the canvas: Ippo Gala, round two, KO; Michael Luna, KO in the first round (announcer: "Everywhere you go, they ask about Manny Pacquiao. He is young, he is colorful, and he keeps busy inside the ring"); Wook-Ki Lee, April 24, 1997 on ESPN, a KO in round one (announcer: "The shot to the body might have broken the Korean's ribs!"). The crowd whooped it up, always sensing blood. And so it went.

3

THE BLACK NAZARENE

MANNY PACQUIAO has visions. He dreams of God. Many of his religious dreams—for him, tactile and real—center around an altar at the Quiapo Church where the sounds of cars and the smell of exhaust fumes swirl around worshippers. The Quiapo Church is not far from the L&M Gym. Pacquiao passes the heaps of trash and the women selling rosaries, and prays there. Signs of Catholicism are everywhere in the Philippines. Morning Mass takes place in shopping malls, in alleys, in the trash dumps, but Quiapo creates something particularly mystical in Pacquiao's mind. In his early days in Manila, Pacquiao would bow his head and then look up at the Black Nazarene. *Nuestro Padre de Jesus Nazareno.* It is a wooden Christ sculpture crowned in thorns and created by an unidentified Mexican artist. The Black Nazarene came to Manila under mysterious circumstances some four hundred years ago. A priest brought it from Mexico on a galleon bound for the Philippines. It arrived in Manila on May 31, 1606. Some people say the ship burned, like a ghost ship, and the Nazarene turned black, but the Christ figure didn't burn. *The first miracle.* In

1621, the fanaticism over the sculpture was so great that the Filipinos formed a society of devotees to protect and honor the idol. The society continues today, and among its greatest devotees is one Manny Pacquiao.

People come by the hundreds of thousands to pray before the Black Nazarene and try to find a personal connection to God. Heads bowed, the rosaries shake in their hands. They push toward the image, aching to touch his body, which has been sprinkled with rose oil, or wanting to put a finger on his hair, hair that was donated from the heads of Chinese women. Or they try to place their human finger on the maroon robe, which protects the Black Nazarene's wooden flesh. Any contact brings miracles, they say. Christ is in a semi-kneeling position, as if straining to get up, like someone with lower-back issues. (There *is* a cross on his back.) His eyes express pain, but determination. Faith in the idol *brings miracles. . . . It cures fatal illnesses.* Through the years Quiapo has experienced fires, earthquakes, and World War II carpet bombing. The Nuestro Padre de Jesus Nazareno survived unscathed. On January 9, every year, a procession starts at the Church and then . . . *pandemonium.* The devotees, who must sign up for a thirty-year stint, carry the Black Nazarene through the Manila streets. Every year, people die in the chaos, like in Pamplona with the running of the bulls.

Filipinos talk of God constantly. They identify with the suffering of Jesus. That is why on Black Saturdays—the traditional Easter Vigil in the Philippines—men dressed as Roman centurions nail people to crosses. They hammer through the believers' palms. Although they are having a five-inch nail go through their hands, the "Jesuses" don't flinch—that would be a sign of laughable weakness; they are suffering only momentary pain for their sins. (These men who act out the crucifixation *are* human, so sometimes they collapse from blood loss, and they are nonchalantly carried away.) This fanaticism goes way back. Christianity took hold in the 1500s, rapidly replacing indigenous beliefs because the belief system was written down in the "Holy Book"—and it promised eternal life. "They believe, we believe, that everything we do is not our own doing," a Filipino friend who knows Pacquiao told me. "That a higher being was in control of what's happening around us; this was even before the concept of Christ came to the Philippines. Maybe it is something innate within Filipinos. I have met a lot of people who have come from nothing, became something else, and all of a sudden forgot where they came from. Manny is still kind and God-fearing." During Holy Week, the country essentially shuts down as religious processions weave their way through the streets of Manila with floats that show the stations of the cross, Judas betraying Jesus, et cetera. When the floats are brought back to their neighborhoods for viewing, people raid the floats' ferns or flowers, thinking they are holy and God is within the objects. One of the most popular T-shirts on Manila streets has an outline of Manny Pacquiao, arms outstretched, praying before a fight. Pacquiao's image looks exactly like Christ on the cross.

Manny Pacquiao is constantly crossing himself and praying. "God is always with me," Pacquiao, looking at me in a sort of trance, once told me. "When I grew up, my mother taught me how to pray and believe in God. You have to trust God and believe in God. If you feel nervous or you feel doubt, you don't feel good. I show my belief in God through confidence. If you believe . . . you don't feel nervous." He then rose from his seat and serenely strolled away.

PACQUIAO'S FAITH has matured during his twenties and into his thirties. When he was a young boxer in Manila, his belief was more of a self-help tool used to give him psychological power in the boxing ring. As Pacquiao's success increased (he was now sharing a small room, instead of sleeping in the L&M's boxing ring), so did his abilities to get into personal trouble. Whether drinking, fighting in a bar, or engaging in other nefarious activities, the money in his pocket was fueling an over-confidence in his psyche. He is known for his tremendous humility, but a boxer must also have unshakeable confidence. His life depends on feeling superior to the other guy in the ring. ("Fighters have to believe they are better than anyone," says Sugar Ray Leonard. "I had the same thing: it's a confidence that is borderline arrogant.") Pacquiao's journey to his current psychological superiority was hard-fought and complicated. Pacquiao wasn't capitalizing on the richest tradition of boxing success.

The Filipino boxing community regularly refers to the great Pancho Villa, who fought in the *1920s*. But given his 19–1 (11 TKOs) professional record and fan appeal, Pacquiao was given a chance to begin a similar journey to greatness at the Oriental and Pacific Boxing Federation (OPBF) flyweight title in his favorite venue, in Mandaluyong. Pacquiao would try and take the belt from Chokchai Chockvivat (34–2), a twenty-nine-year-old Thai fighter (aka Chokchai 3K Battery) who had held the belt for four years.

Pacquiao (now twenty and still growing—he was five feet four) had knocked out his last seven opponents. He was thin as a bamboo stick and wasn't very active with his footwork. His right jab was lazy and ineffectual against someone of the Thai's skills. Pacquiao decided to close in and slug it out a couple of times to the consternation of the ringside aficionados and the ESPN Asia crew. Pacquiao finally settled into moving clumsily around the ring, as his opponent kept cutting him off. As the fight progressed, Pacquiao's jab didn't improve, but he became better at attacking. His left hand could cause serious damage, but his weak right-glove position was allowing Chokchai to land counterpunches. *Manny Pacquiao can't withstand many more relentless punches to the midsection for very much longer. I think Manny Pacquiao is a little fragile in the midsection.* Pacquiao was wincing at every body shot. The Thai was starting to control the fight, throwing big rights. Pacquiao was losing the fight to the Asian champion who had held the belt since 1993. But at 2:46 into round five, Manny boxed his opponent into the corner, led with a soft right and then hit him with a ferocious left. Chokchai was slumped in the corner, totally destroyed, and Pacquiao had won the flyweight title. The fans, of course, went ballistic.

Even with the championship, Pacquiao was still on the bottom of the boxing pyramid. One time, a television crew was setting up for one of Pacquiao's fights. It was late, and they had been working hard all day. A person from Pacquiao's contingent came over and sat down and started chowing down with the crew. They let him, of course, but he had invited himself, and they viewed it as rude. Pacquiao sat in a corner and observed the whole scene. He was really, really hungry, but he had too much pride to join them. He couldn't afford to eat. Someone noticed him and invited him to come over, too. He reluctantly did so.

IN PACQUIAO'S FIRST OPBF flyweight title defense, he went against another Thai and beat him in the first round. Then Pacquiao traveled to Tokyo for a first round TKO of Shin Terao, a Japanese fighter, and then flew to the outskirts of Bangkok to take on Chatchai Sasakul for the World Boxing Council (WBC) flyweight title. Sasakul, who had five years of experience in significant fights, had lost only once, to Yuri Arbachakov, who many considered a top pound-for-pound fighter. Pacquiao, meanwhile, had contested only two twelve-rounders against Chokchai Chockvivat and Panomdej Ohyuthanakorn, and neither had gone the distance. Going from an OPBF titlist to a WBC match is akin to going in baseball from AA to the big leagues, or a second division club to the Premier League in soccer. Pacquiao worked out and trained with Asi Taulava, a popular Filipino pro basketball player. The title bout was to be held in an outside venue, on December 4, 1998. Only the six-member *Blow by Blow* television crew, which had begged and pleaded with higher-ups into letting them cover the fight, were attending it along with hundreds of Thais. It was a muggy day, the sort of Thai weather that leads to long naps and lots of cold beer. Sasakul, grim-faced, was undefeated in thirty-five fights, and early on exposed Pacquiao's lack of technical boxing skills. Sasakul schooled Pacquiao for six rounds, but Pacquiao accepted the punishment, banging his green gloves together in vain determination, biting his lower lip. In round seven, both men bounced around the ring and came toward each other in spurts. In round eight, Sasakul wanted to make an early night of it, so he went on the offensive. *Pacquiao has got to be careful! It's a brawl. What a fight!* Then Pacquiao moved forward, and Sasakul counterpunched. It felt like a trap, but his speed proved to be too much. Pacquiao hit Sasakul with a vicious left to the jaw. Pacquiao's quick hands stunned the Thai, and then Pacquiao slipped in a straight left. Sasakul went face first onto the canvas. There was an outpouring of glee from the Filipinos. The Thais were grasping to understand what had just happened. ("We were lucky to get out of there alive," says one Pinoy who attended the bout.) After the fight, observers could see the teeth marks in Pacquiao's lower lip where he had practically bit through it.

The WBC flyweight title was regarded as Pacquiao's first significant win. In Southeast Asia, Pacquiao was making a name for himself, but when it came right down to it, he was only a regional phenomenon. Asian fighters were lightly regarded worldwide because they hadn't really fought against world class competition, and anyone watching the fight could respect Pacquiao's speed and his left hand but could also see that he could be out-boxed.

His first title defense was against Gabriel Mira from Argentina. Pacquiao ran in the early mornings and then worked out at the L&M gym in the afternoons. Throughout his career, Pacquiao has had a tendency to call his shots. "As soon as I see an opening, I will go for the knockout," said Pacquiao, confidently, in the pre-fight press conference. In round four, Pacquiao nailed Mira with a left to the jaw for a standing eight count. Mira was knocked down again almost immediately. Then, for some reason or another, he got back up. And with a lunging left, Pacquiao put him to sleep to retain the title.

Pacquiao was having issues with his body. Remaining at flyweight (between 108 and 112 pounds) had become impossible. A healthier diet had initiated a late growth spurt (in the next few years, he would grow two inches), and his suddenly fuller frame was creating weight problems. He was set to travel to Thailand to take on Medgoen Singsurat, also known as Medgoen 3K Battery because the Thai Storage Battery Public Company Limited had asked him to change his name for a fee. Pacquiao, twenty-one, starved himself for days leading up to the fight, but he couldn't make the 112-pound weight limit, and he lost his WBC Flyweight title at the weigh-in, and as another penalty for being overweight, he was forced to use a different type of glove. He (and his handlers) had placed him into an impossible situation. Pacquiao made it to round three. Exhausted and dehydrated, he was KO'd with a body shot that some detractors would call a shadow punch.

After the loss, Pacquiao moved up to super bantamweight. Given that matchmakers realized that Pacquiao was growing and that he was still an improving and bankable boxer, he was given a shot at the WBC international bantamweight title at the Elorde Sports Complex (the one that is now mostly used as a cockfighting arena) against Reynante Jamili. Pacquiao won with a TKO in round two.

Pacquiao then defended the title in March 2000 against Arnel Barotillo in the Ninoy Aquino Stadium in Manila. He destroyed Barotillo with a scary right in round four. Barotillo stood for a second, tried to catch his balance, and then dropped. This was followed by a first round TKO against Seung-Kon Chae. He threw a left uppercut to reduce Seung-Kon Chae to dreamland. Pacquiao crossed himself, as if to say, "That one is for you, God," and the crowd went crazy.

Moving up in even just one weight class can make a fighter seem small and weak. But Pacquiao had yet to take on a super bantamweight that could outclass him.

While Manny Pacquiao is now called the best boxer in the world, he has not always dominated his opponents, including some that were evidently inferior. On October 14, 2000, Pacquiao took on Nedal Hussein in a half-filled Ynares Sports Center in Antipolo City, the Philippines. Filipinos were hardly gracious hosts to Hussein, who is known as Skinny. Maybe they were worried. Before the fight, Skinny's record read 19–0 (11 KOs) to Pacquiao's 29–2 (20 KOs).

Skinny was put up three hours away from the venue in a one-star hotel. "Wasn't pleasant, that was for sure," says Hussein, an Australian. "But if you can't handle the challenge, you shouldn't be a boxer."

In the first four rounds, Hussein dominated Pacquiao. Then Pacquiao started outboxing Hussein. "He had a reputation as a bit of a gambler, and someone who drank more than he should have, but he had stamina," Hussein told me between selling used cars at Knockout Autos in Sydney. In the fourth round, Pacquiao walked into an ordinary jab and fell to his knees. The count went to *eighteen* seconds. Pacquiao, brain throbbing, was visibly hurt, gasping for oxygen and equilibrium. The crowd was silent, arms crossed. As Skinny went in for the kill, Pacquiao desperately held on. Hussein couldn't get Pacquiao off him and tried to muscle him away. He accidentally elbowed him. "Just trying to push him off, to be honest," says Skinny. Carlos Padilla Jr., a Filipino referee who had worked the "Thrilla in Manila," deducted one point. After the long count and the iffy deduction, Hussein was rightly livid. He nodded fatefully as if to say, "This is sorta fucked up." Pacquiao was tired. The hometown announcers were calling Hussein a dirty fighter, but it was Pacquiao who was wrapping his elbow around the Aussie's neck, trying not to fall down. As the fight wore on, Pacquaio, clad in black trunks, recovered well and started outboxing his opponent. In round seven, Hussein, now the exhausted boxer, bull-rushed Pacquiao and knocked him down.

Between the ninth and tenth rounds, the fans threw bottles into the ring. In round ten, Skinny had a cut, not too serious, on his cheek, and Padilla stopped the fight. It was a premature stoppage. "I felt cheated by the referee," says Hussein. "As long as the fighters keep fighting, let them fight." (Hussein made $8,000 for his controversial loss, while Pacquiao soared to fame and fortune. Hussein still feels robbed but expresses no bitterness toward Pacquiao, who he says has developed into an even "better offensive fighter, he is smarter, and more disciplined and dedicated.")

At the end of the controversial fight, Pacquiao seemed more relieved than giddy. He was still a world champion, but barely. He hadn't even gone against the true class in his division, which were Mexicans and Americans.

After stopping Tetsutora Senrima (a North Korean living in Japan) in Antipolo City and Thailand's Wethya Sakmuang-klang in a jam-packed Kidapawan provincial gymnasium, Pacquiao's life would take an unusual twist.

THE FILIPINO migration starts in the countryside. Pacquiao knew many people who had left the country for something else. "Help Wanted" signs are nailed to coconut trees everywhere. The people, 10 percent of whom leave the Philippines, move through Manila to Saudi Arabia, Kuwait, the United States, *two hundred* other countries. (A war correspondent friend of mine, who has spent a lot of time in Afghanistan, told me the only people he has seen smile in that wretched country are the Filipino workers, who do the worst of the country's chores.) The Filipino Diaspora goes through Manila Bay, where people are herded onto ferries, or through the Ninoy Aquino Airport. There is not really a romantic term for the leaving. The national rite is the subject of books, television, and movies, and obsessed over by all. Leaving is part of being Pinoy. But the people who leave are simply OFWs—Overseas Filipino Workers.

Rod Nazario, Pacquiao's manager, happened to be leaving for the United States to visit family members in California. Pacquiao heard about the trip and expressed an interest in joining him. Nazario told him he could come, and maybe they could find a prize fight. In retrospect, Nazario told the story like it all came by happenstance, but he had a quiet plan. "If I can bring Pacquiao to the U.S., he will be the most popular boxer in the United States," he told someone at the L&M. No one really believed the old promoter. Nazario felt like Pacquiao had a natural ability, but he needed more polish, which he couldn't get in the Philippines. "I could tell there was something inside him, but he had not yet discovered it because no one was teaching him."

4

THE WILD CARD BOXING CLUB

ON A MONDAY in February 2010, Manny Pacquiao arrived at 1123 Vine Street, Los Angeles, got out of his black SUV, breast-stroking his way through the dozens of adoring Filipinos. Ten minutes earlier the Wild Card Boxing Club had been cleared, except for Pacquiao's entourage, gym employees, sparring partners, his trainers, and a couple cops who talked their way into the joint. The Wild Card—the most renowned gym on the West Coast, possibly in the world—has hardly changed from the first time he arrived in 2001, except Pacquiao has turned from a broomstick to The Man. For the next few hours, the Wild Card will revolve around him.

The boys in the entourage know the hierarchy, know that Freddie and Alex will put Manny through the paces, know each of them will have their own remarkably trivial role. They stand at the ready to towel, spritz, laugh, joke with, protect, hold his cell phone, get him a new T-shirt, endure him slapping them (hard) in the face as a prank, and spraying them with his water bottle. To the great envy of their countrymen, the Filipino news corps will send these fun-loving images back to the Philippines. Buboy Fernandez, the most recognizable of the entourage, sweats profusely as he hits the heavy bag. Pacquiao has always wanted to help people and to bring "home" with him everywhere he goes in the world. When he was a young boxer in Manila, he returned to General Santos City for a visit. Pacquiao noticed a young man sitting in the street, who looked strung out. He knew the boy, Restituto "Buboy" Fernandez, well—they had been neighbors, their shacks separated by a piece of wood. Pacquiao took Fernandez, whose only income came as a part-time fish deliveryman, away from the street. He told him, "Come with me, and I will give you a job as a trainer." Fernandez was reluctant, but Pacquiao brought him to Manila. By all accounts, including Fernandez's, Pacquiao saved his life. Buboy, whose waistline could benefit from fewer slices of Spam, is still Manny's best friend. He works Manny's corner along with Freddie Roach. Buboy tends to shake his head in bewilderment at the entourage, Manny's political ambitions, and other antics, but he is helpless to control any of it. Buboy, a genial companion, tells me his life goal is to protect his friend, but the only place where he feels he has this power is in the ring. The other nonsense is completely out of his control, and he can just barely tolerate it. Freddie Roach relies on Fernandez implicitly. He will joke around that Buboy knows nothing about boxing and then turn serious and say, "I couldn't do this without him." Between rounds, Roach gives Pacquiao strategy in English, which Buboy translates into Visyan. During fights, Buboy, who has won multiple trainer-of-the-year honors in the Philippines, carefully studies the opponent's tendencies and screeches them to Pacquiao in the cadence of an auctioneer.

Buboy can become overwrought during a fight and if Pacquiao looks like he is in trouble, he will start crying uncontrollably. Roach has had to calm him down several times during championship bouts. He keeps walloping the bag with great aim and eventually lumbers to the corner, near the speed bags.

The people without any duties at the Wild Card Boxing Club are doing a tremendous amount of horse trading in Pacquiao memorabilia—signed gloves, posters, and other stuff is getting moved around like crazy; half of it will be on eBay before nightfall. Everyone tries to make money off Pacquiao, who always seems to be wearily signing things. It is the Pacquiao pyramid, and it is unclear how he is profiting from the black market.

Pacquiao finally saunters in to the club and makes a beeline toward Freddie Roach, his Parkinson's disease–afflicted trainer. "Fred-eeeeeee Roach. The world's greatest trainerrrrr."

"Manny Pacquiao." Roach smiles. Boxing historians place the Pacquiao-Roach partnership among the elite of the sport's all-time fighter-trainer connections, along with Muhammad Ali and Angelo Dundee, Joe Louis and Jack "Chappie" Blackburn, Joe Frazier and Eddie Futch, Emile Griffith and Gil Clancy, and Thomas Hearns and Emanuel Steward. ("It's magic," says the promoter Bob Arum, the chairman of the boxing promotions company Top Rank Boxing. "Made in heaven. They're so in tune with each other, it's like watching a ballet.")

Freddie hasn't seen Pacquiao for a couple days because the coach had been working someone else's corner on Saturday night.

"Happy?"

"First round knockout," says Roach, nodding.

Pacquiao tells Roach that a journalist had given him a ride to the gym. "He's a valet."

"I know him, it's okay."

They laugh.

"How was your workout yesterday?"

"Good. We went twelve rounds; we ran hills."

There is a secret understanding between them. They nod.

Pacquiao goes into the closetlike locker room to change into his workout clothes and gets his hands wrapped.

SOMETHING is wrong with Freddie Roach. His movements are a beat or two off-sync; the occasional phrase or sentence is interrupted by an abrupt pause, then a marble-mouthed slurring. He has tremors that are so forceful that they wake him up by 6 a.m. He has drop-foot (his left foot drags with each step), arthritis in both elbows, and cervical dystonia (muscle contractions in the neck). These are all from Parkinson's, the body snatcher. Roach is a complex soul, a man who has given his life to boxing.

"It all started in the back *yawd*, in Dedham," he told me several years ago. There is a class divide in Dedham, Massachusetts: Upper Dedham, where the rich folk live, and East Dedham, home of the housing projects. Freddie was an East Dedham kid. The Roaches were Irish and French-Canadian; his dad, Paul, was the New England featherweight champion in 1947, and fanatical about having his boys follow him into the fight game. He built them a ring in the backyard. At eight years of age, Freddie woke at 6 a.m. to do road work, ran his paper route after school, ate dinner, took a bus to the gym and trained, and got back home at eleven. He would take Friday off, but Saturday and Sunday were travel days. Dad, a "working stiff" tree cutter, would take him and his brothers to gyms in the area. Freddie had talent but he was mostly a hard-worker who wanted to please his old man. "If you kept him happy, there would be less beatings; he was a physical person," says Freddie, who had 150 amateur fights. "If you boxed, he liked you, and you wanted to keep him happy." Freddie's oldest brother, Pepper, the most talented of the five Roach boys, was also the favorite, but when he quit the ring at age fifteen he was immediately kicked out of the house. "My dad was just a mean guy," says Freddie.

Roach, known as "Choir Boy," went pro in 1978. During the 1980s, he was a popular fighter on ESPN's Thursday night fights (one of his matches, a particularly brutal affair against Tommy Cordova, was named "Fight of the Year"), but his biggest payday netted him a mere $13,000. Freddie could box, but once he was hit, the fight was on; he couldn't control himself. He was a give-and-take type guy, a white kid who fought hard and bled easily. Roach trained under Eddie Futch, a soft-spoken man, considered one of the best trainers to ever whisper in fighter's ears. An old boxing hand who trained with Joe Louis in the 1930s, Futch sculpted the strategy of the first two boxers (Joe Frazier and Ken Norton) to defeat Muhammad Ali. Ranked as high as number six in the junior featherweight division, Roach was one fight away from a WBA bantamweight title shot when he broke and tore tendons in his right hand, an injury from which he would never recover. And then, fatally, he fought before he was ready. And he lost brutally. Futch told the Choir Boy to hang up his gloves. Roach, who was twenty-six at the time, wept, and then ignored the sage advice. He believes his decision to continue boxing contributed to the onslaught of Parkinson's, much like Ali. Roach fought four more times and took too many blows. He finally retired in October 1986 after fifty-four pro bouts. He absorbed punishment for a total of 406 rounds. Freddie had written into his ESPN contract that his father, Paul, would be flown to all of his bouts. "I remember, in the dressing room, when I retired, he said, 'What happened?' And I said, 'What do you mean, What happened?' I had just retired on TV; I knew that I wouldn't fight again. I didn't try to win; I was really embarrassed to be in the ring. I knew at that moment I would never fight again. And he asked me, 'What happened?' And, I said, 'What do you mean, what happened?' 'How could you go from being so good to now?' I said, 'I don't fucking know.' When I got mad, I swore at him a little bit. I yelled at him a little bit. I felt bad about that. I never apologized. He died shortly after that. It seems like when I gave up boxing, he kind of gave up life. He didn't socialize, didn't really have any outlets. Just stayed at home, smoking cigarettes and getting old."

When Roach retired from the ring, he was broke; he owed back taxes, and he didn't have a job so he became a telemarketer, hawking coffee mugs and key tags with two of his four brothers, Joey and Pepper—both former fighters, as all Roach men were. The soft-spoken ex-pugilist was a lousy salesman. He boozed and put on forty-five pounds. He got into brawls on the Las Vegas Strip. Bitter and in financial trouble, he relaxed one day by going to see Futch who worked out of a Las Vegas gym. Roach was hanging around when he started watching Virgil Hill spar with someone. Roach knew Hill, and when he noticed no one was really paying attention to the fighter, he got close to the apron, gave Hill a drink of water, and offered him a little advice. Hill liked what he heard and ended up hiring Roach, who has a reputation as a master tactician, who understands temperamental fighters (he trained Mike Tyson for two fights), and doesn't seek the limelight. Roach showed up at the gym every day, and by the next year he was Futch's most trusted assistant. On September 7, 1987, Hill won the WBA light heavyweight title by TKO with Roach in his corner. It was the first world championship for them both. "I have been doing this for so long that it's like second nature to me," says Roach who works from 8 a.m. to 8 p.m. six days a week, taking off Sundays for a movie and dinner. Roach was engaged once, but he has never married because women "don't understand that boxing is my first priority," he says. "My philosophy: Some trainers like to scream and yell, maybe motivate their fighters that way, but I feel nobody responds well to yelling. No one likes to be screamed at. So I think I get more out of them by being their friend and being quiet with them. When they come to the corner I have them take a couple deep breaths so they can calm down, and then they are going to absorb what I am going to say to them, and I am not going to say too much. Some guys want to write a book in the corner, but if a fighter can absorb one or two things, that's what I'm looking for." (Boxer Bernard Hopkins, once a charge of Roach's, told *Sports Illustrated*, "There are too many damn trainers and not enough teachers. There's a twenty-mile difference between some trainer and a teacher. Freddie Roach is a teacher.")

In 1991, Roach came to Los Angeles to work with actor and light heavyweight boxer Mickey Rourke. He lived in Rourke's Outlaw Gym at Hollywood and Highland. He trained Rourke, who Roach calls a very good "fool around fighter," until the actor gave it up. After the Outlaw Gym went away, Roach was determined to control his own fate. He leased a strip club on Vine Street, which he turned into his gym. (During the renovation he had to remove two stripper poles.)

There isn't much to it on a regular day except fifty or so sinewy men with marbled deltoid muscles packed into a room in the rundown, Hollywood strip mall. During the regular sparring sessions, Roach stands in the ringside corner and chews his fingernails. Underneath the pictures of world champions whom Freddie has trained—Tyson, Pacquiao, De La Hoya, Bernard Hopkins, James Toney, and Wladimir Klitschko, to name just a few—there is always a shitload of movement: It's loud with Filipinos, Russians, Mexicans, Puerto Ricans, and African Americans jump-roping, shadow-boxing, speed-bagging, heavy-bag hitting, and the more mundane goings-on—fighters putting on groin protectors, gloves, and tape, and chit-chatting with the champions and down-and-out ex-fighters who hang out there. They all have the happy and self-enclosed look of people who love being in the gym and find difficulties dealing with the world outside of its walls. There's Pepper, a recovered meth addict and an ex-con, who tries to make sure everyone is okay. As reported by *Vanity Fair*'s Peter Owen Nelson, on his rap sheet is a vehicle identification theft scam. But he is always willing to help someone and loves showing off a photo of his wife and kids. Pepper is performing mitt-man duties ("Um-ma, HA! Um-ma, HA!"). The Wild Card's security guy, Rob can barely contain himself when the door is left open. He wants to make sure no heat leaves the gym.

Roach isolates himself (as much as possible) in the corner, underneath a sign that philosophizes: IT TAKES BALLS TO RULE THE WORLD. Generous to a fault, he has a handful of hundreds in his pocket, and men come up to him and sometimes he will slip them a bill to help hold them over until their next fight. He is known as a good guy, but rival managers and their fans don't always like him. In 2004, he was forced to pay $10,000 after he punched out a Kinko's customer who threatened him. "I said to him, 'If you take another step, I'm gonna knock you out,'" Roach recalls, "Motherfuckers always take that step." Whenever a fist is waved in Roach's face, he will think. "Don't forget Kinko's." Roach has a suspicious mentality about finance. When his lawyer took him to a Wells Fargo branch to open a checking account, Roach was hesitant: "Can we really trust these guys?" Men pat him on the back, and spit into a red bucket next to him, but for all the attention, it's obvious that he is in his own world, studying—through his nerd glasses—the carnage in the ring. In a sport where irrationality is endemic, there is intelligence in Freddie's eyes. He concentrates on his fighters, which seems to lighten the constant pain in his own body. ("Saw a neurosurgeon the other day, he told me about a brain surgery, but I am still functioning on the meds pretty well.") He wears a Michael J. Fox Foundation T-shirt. He takes three kinds of medication daily, and he is injected with Botox to treat his dystonia, which has been likened to constantly having a charley horse in your neck. But he won't let people talk about it or feel sorry for him.

"Give 'em the double jab," he mouths.

USED TO BE that neighborhood gyms created a grassroots interest in boxing: People appreciated the skills of a boxer because they used boxing gyms, like a modern health club, to stay in shape. You could also run into the local stars and watch a young Joe Louis or Cassius Clay get their work in, or go to New York's Gramercy Gym to see one of Floyd Patterson's legendary workouts. When Freddie was a kid, his old man would take him over to Brockton where Marvin Hagler trained at the Petronelli brothers' gym. That sort of torch passing and camaraderie exists only in a handful of places in America anymore. The decline started fifty years ago.

Boxing is one of the only sports known to man which television hurt. As A. J. Liebling wrote dismissively, four or five decades ago, television was "an electronic gadget that peddles razor blades." Back in the 1950s, the networks started putting boxing on television, which made the sport more widely known, but it also helped to kill it because people stopped going to local smoker bouts. Intimate smokers, where the boxers learned their trade, also benefited the clubs because they would help promote the fights. When the smokers started going away, so did the clubs, and the level of boxing declined, too. But television was only the first blow. Boxing has always had problems with feuding organizers, corrupt promoters, the mob, and an increasingly more educated society. "Boxing in this country has suffered long from a reputation acquired by association with the wrong kind of men—not all of them, of course, but enough to make it bad," read a newspaper article about reforming the sport. The year? 1917. But it remained one of America's three major sports into the 1950s.

Despite its image, boxing was a semi-major sport in the United States until the 1980s when there came a slow decline. "Used to be that the Golden Gloves and the Police Athletic League were big," says Hall of Famer Sugar Ray Leonard, who thinks boxing needs to invest in the grassroots. "It's a dark time in American boxing." Televised poker, it could be convincingly argued, is more popular. For the last five years, boxing is under yet another, and potentially lethal, threat called mixed martial arts. The MMA is an almost-anything-goes blood sport that combines boxing, wrestling, and martial arts. Until about ten years ago, it was outlawed in the United States. But the Ultimate Fighting Championship (UFC), a company out of Las Vegas, bought the brand, reformed it, and made Dana White its president. White is a media-friendly former boxing manager turned UFC impresario. He has brokered television deals, created reality shows, and promotes his sport like it is a major sports enterprise. It plays well to white American audiences because most of the fighters are white. With its now recognizable stars, fast action, and better organization, much of the public's fight dollars, and interest, are flowing toward the UFC.

Freddie Roach knows about mixed martial arts, and he trains a UFC world champion or two and other MMA fighters who come to learn boxing from him, but Roach doesn't like the sport. He thinks the fighters "punch like girls," and he feels that boxing is more strategic; it is an art passed on for generations, and it "looks better." But what will all these forces mean to the future of boxing? Roach, fifty, wonders.

THE WILD CARD is a throwback to another era. There are elements of Hollywood (the actors Christian Bale and Mark Wahlberg work out at the club), but most of the people paying their daily five dollar fee are looking for a way out, some are looking to protect themselves on the streets, some want to look tough, and some want a cessation of their grief. They are the ones making noise. The pros come during the day; they are quieter. They are working on skills and strategy.

"That's my favorite sign," Roach says, pointing to the words: *Everyone here seems normal until you get to know them.*

Roach, an optimist, opened the gym in the hope that a world champion prospect would walk through the door. And one day he did.

IN 2001, an undernourished Filipino kid came into that gym. Freddie was in the ring working the mitts, and a man named Mr. Nazario approached him. Everyone thinks they can be a world champion, but Roach can size someone up within seconds. He didn't know Rod Nazario, a man's man who, as one Filipino journalist wrote after Nazario's death, did "great things quietly, almost in secret." If someone needed help, like someone needing a room, Nazario would serendipitously arrange it, silently slipping the person a room key. Roach had no idea how they had ended up in his gym, but ten days earlier Nazario had arrived in the United States with Pacquiao.

Manny knew Nazario was coming to the United States, called him, and asked if he could join him. They first went to San Francisco to see Nazario's son, and Pacquiao went to a gym in the East Bay, but he didn't like it. After two days in the Bay Area, they took a bus to Los Angeles. They stayed with Nazario's nephew who still comes to Pacquiao's fights, and even has a cupboard in his kitchen filled with Gatorade, *just in case* Pacquiao stops by to say hello. Then Nazario put him in a boarding house, about a mile from the Wild Card. They decided to visit the gym one day. Freddie was standing in the middle of the ring, holding the punch mitts. Nazario buttered up Freddie by telling him that he heard that Roach was great at catching punches and then pointed to Pacquiao with a biographical sketch:

"I have a WBC international titlist," said Nazario.

"Let him suit up," said Freddie. Later, he admitted, "I had never heard of him. *No idea* who this guy was."

THERE IS something about working the mitts with a fighter. It's an unwritten understanding between fighter and trainer, not unlike being comfortable with a dance partner. No one had ever reacted to and anticipated Manny's punches so well. Featherweights make their living on quickness, but Roach noticed the explosion of the punches: "The speed and power worked so well together. Kind of just jumped on you." He could feel the "very, very sharp punches," through the mitts. Although he tended to get off balance after a combination, Pacquiao's footwork was also exemplary. "Within three minutes, it was like we knew each other our entire lives," says Roach. "At the end of that first session, Roach went over to his people and he said, "Wow, this guy can fucking fight." Pacquiao went to his manager and said, "Boss. We have a new trainer." It was the first time Pacquiao had approved of a trainer.

There is a secret language in the gym, one of shared experiences born of poverty, whether in Mindanao or Dedham. "It's the language of boxing, more or less," says Roach. "I think he knows I have Parkinson's because it has been so publicized, but for the first five or six years, he had no clue. We don't talk about that stuff. Our relationship is more boxing. More father-son."

STEP ONE was complete, but Pacquiao also needed representation, which is always a difficult task in boxing because managers control a boxer's finances. Considering that most boxers leave their careers without a penny, managers are sometimes seen as rather shady characters. But Pacquiao needed an American promoter, so Rod Nazario met Murad Muhammad at the Vagabond Inn, which is next door to the Wild Card. Nazario put in a tape of Pacquiao knocking out Chokchai Chockvivat, as Muhammad watched. He had been around the American fight game for decades. Convinced of Pacquiao's potential, Muhammed started working on getting Pacquiao a prizefight. As it happened, Lehlohonolo Ledwaba of South Africa, the International Boxing Federation (IBF) junior featherweight title holder, was scheduled to defend his title in ten days. His opponent, Hector Velasquez, was cut during training, and so Pacquiao's name came up. Nazario was about ready to get on a plane for Manila, but he returned from the airport to sign the contract for Manny. "Had I left then, Murad would have gone off and looked for another fighter," Nazario said.

Pacquiao was just a slender—almost gangly—kid, 121 pounds, but full of ambition. It was his first time in Las Vegas. The fight would take place well before the headliner as the night's star was to be Oscar De La Hoya. The Golden Boy was nine years from winning an Olympic gold medal and trying to regain his ambition for boxing. De La Hoya, at 154 pounds, would win a unanimous twelve-round decision against Javier Castillejo of Spain, capturing Castillejo's World Boxing Council super welterweight championship and join Sugar Ray Leonard and Thomas Hearns as the only boxers to win world titles in five weight classes. De La Hoya, twenty-eight, would be the youngest to accomplish this feat, but his fight was an artless snoozefest. Much of the post-fight chatter was about the Pacquiao-Ledwaba fight. It was Manny Pacquiao versus Lehlohonolo Ledwaba for the IBF super bantamweight title; June 23, 2001, at the MGM Grand. Pacquiao (32–2, 23 KOs) had reddish hair, like a fox, and a thin mustache. Ledwaba, twenty-nine, was five years older (33–1–1, 22 KOs), but they were essentially the same size, five feet five and 121 pounds.

Pacquiao wore black trunks; Ledwaba wore white, which were soon to be drenched in blood.

To prepare Pacquiao, Roach had quickly assembled a platoon of Mexican sparring partners. Pacquiao, then twenty-two, told friends that he would come out from the bell in a "fullout war." "I expect him to beat Ledwaba. He's quicker and stronger," said Roach before the fight. "Manny hits harder than any fighter I know in his division. The difference in the fight will be speed. Manny can't stand in front of Ledwaba because he'll get hit. He's got to use his footspeed and look for angles." Trainers always try and pump their charges with confidence; Ledwaba was a prohibitive favorite and most observers thought he would crush Manny. Pacquiao never gave Ledwaba a chance to breathe. He had yet to learn how to attack his opponent at sharp and unpredictable angles, but his speed was difficult for even a seasoned boxer to handle.

"Beautiful Manny," Freddie Roach said at the end of the first round. "Deep breath. . . . More head movement, like in the locker room. When you fake him, he's going to reach, and it's going to open him up. Okay? Go with the straight left hand and the hook behind it."

At the end of round four, Ledwaba was hurt with a short right hook, not even Manny's best punch.

Pacquiao crossed himself going into the sixth round, and forty seconds later Ledwaba was on his butt, finding it difficult to regain his balance. Twenty seconds later, Manny nailed him with a left, and Ledwaba crumpled. Roach was laughing.

"We got a winner!" shouted Murad Muhammad, sitting ringside. Boxing historian Bert Sugar sat next to the promoter that night. ("A big character, but he didn't know much about boxing," says Sugar, who marveled at the twin women on the promoter's arms.)

Manny Pacquiao was the new IBF super bantamweight champion. He had come to the United States on a whim, and now he was a world champion. No Filipino had ever won a world title under the glitz of the Las Vegas lights.

"I never expected it to be this tough," said Ledwaba, who suffered only his second loss. "I was surprised by the knockdown in the second round; it was a total shock. He came on really hard. He just caught me in the last round."

"I was the aggressor," Pacquiao said.

He went back to Manila and was greeted with the fanfare of someone who had just visited a neighboring planet, meeting with the president of the country—who gave him one million pesos—and riding through the streets like a conquering hero.

5

ENTOURAGE

MANNY PACQUIAO'S entourage could easily be called the most ridiculous in sports history. People advise him all the time about this bloated group. They want him to shut it down. Pacquiao shrugs them off. He *knows* the entourage is completely dysfunctional. But Pacquiao gets too many laughs from the guys. It is togetherness, like a frat house, Filipino style. Of the people he knows (and many of them appear from nowhere), they are brothers. They sleep at the foot of his bed, which is seen as an honor. Fun times. Manny Pacquiao doesn't really get any privacy. His childhood was one of want: He wants the smells of food on the stove and good cheer, always good cheer. Training camp can be the ultimate grind, but Pacquiao tries to create a jovial atmosphere. After all, it is a vacation for his closest friends, which number in the hundreds now, a sort of two-month getaway from the responsibilities of home and homeland . . . and their wives.

He wants absolutely no solitude, but this has become difficult to control. Upon building his house in General Santos City, he realized he needed to build castle-sized walls because the people were always coming to his house. He constructed a back entrance so he could sneak away. Sometimes when he is training and in his apartment in Los Angeles with the fourteen or thirty men a few inches from him, he hides away in his room. At night he has his security guy clear the place. Lately, when he is in Los Angeles, he has been sneaking over to his Beverly Hills mansion to catch a nap. But his superstitions trump his need for any privacy: His merry men are considered lucky. He can't just throw them out. Rod Nazario used to say that there was an "unseen hand guiding Manny all these years." Manny is so superstitious that he is physically unable to mess with much. He could save some money and have everyone stay at his mansion, but he doesn't want the guys messing up a house reserved for his family, all of whom usually spend the majority of training camp back in the Philippines. Manny never wants the distraction of family—and too much time in the United States also brings tax problems. When he is back in the Philippines, he insists on playing basketball with his old friends, the "guys who helped him when he had nothing." He gives them each $500 after the games. His friends are part of him, and Robin Hood can't just fire Friar Tuck and the boys because of some personality defects. He has become a man of two worlds: in the Philippines one of black-tie dinners and official visits to the president's residence, and in the other hanging with *his* people.

There are the oddballs who are with him at fight time, like the guy who is attempting to breed a lion with a tiger, an arms dealer, and a gambling lord. There are the people who are hanging around—their duties totally unclear. A personal biographer whose work has never seen the light of day. A personal car washer who makes $200 per wash three times a week, even though the place down the street charges $8.99 for a full-service wash. (When an entourage member suggests a less expensive alternative, Pacquiao admonishes the person, warning him never to eliminate a job of someone trying to earn a living.) There's a live-in dog walker and someone who tries to figure out which flavor of Gatorade the champ will desire that day and another guy whose sole duty seems to be to hold an exercise mat until Manny is ready to do his sit-ups. There are poker, chess, and dart companions, guys who laugh at jokes, and guys who dry the champ's legs with a towel when he works out. A few are entrusted with holding suitcases filled with cash. There's a personal photographer and two people (maybe more) who shoot and edit daily videos. Translators who "no speak good English." Drivers, publicists, gofers, and security. A voice coach. An English tutor. There are other layabouts who don't seem to have any duty, except to walk near Pacquiao when he is on stairs so as to catch one of the most nimble humans on the planet in case he falls.

Buboy Fernandez, Pacquiao's closest friend and the highest in the hierarchy, thinks it's ridiculous. But he understands. Buboy is the embodiment of the entire group. Being around Pacquiao has its perks. But back in the Philippines, it also carries danger.

To Manny Pacquiao, his entourage is an indispensable part of his life. "I'm a nice guy. I am generous. They help me stay loose."

In the Philippines, it isn't really easy to be a loner. Families and friends congregate in groups. People flow in and out of homes like a constant block party. And "family" members can be as devious as outsiders: Pacquiao built a grocery store, but so many people simply charged their purchases back to the PacMan, he had to close it. The Philippines is definitely not a good place to have personal space issues. The entourage reflects Pacquiao's cultural makeup. "They are clingy people," says Freddie Roach. But even Filipinos are unsure about Pacquiao's entourage: They worry that someone will sabotage him. Many of the members are friends of friends—people without a real job who have no real skills. For many it comes down to jealousy. Entourage members based in the Philippines get an all-expense paid trip to the United States, hanging out with the country's biggest idol, doing minor tasks, and getting a good paycheck at the end. "You see, Manny, he's always surrounded by people with their hands out. Manny's got a lot of heart," says Alex Ariza, the conditioning coach. "There are mountains of people asking him for tickets, or asking him to fly them here or there. They ask him to invest in businesses, T-shirt companies, or who knows what. They're like vultures."

You could learn a lot about Manny Pacquiao by his entourage, which seems to have a new member every hour. He sees his weakness. "With all the people around me, it's hard to find a real friend, a die-hard person like Freddie," Pacquiao admits. "We're honest. We don't lie to each other. The strategy we share is nothing but the truth. And I'm lucky to have him in my corner." As for everyone else? Part of the time Pacquiao has no idea who half the people even are. They are friends of friends of friends. "It's not really an entourage; it's a crowd," says Bill Caplan, the longtime boxing publicist.

"He just accepts them." Pacquiao fans chalk it up to his child-hood: He likes the security of numbers; he likes being a benevolent father figure. But really, if you're around him enough, you realize it is part obligation, part the need for a circus. They tamp down the pressure as a fight approaches. Pacquiao hosts nightly karaoke parties and encourages the entourage (and other people) to lose 15 percent of their body weight in a weight-loss contest and offers an award of $3,000. Members of the entourage run the contest out of the training camp condo. At one fight, he gave away $250,000 to eighty people. A stupid waste of money, say critics, but Pacquiao wants to develop a better health system in his coun-try, and he wants to promote healthier habits. He figures the contest will encourage Filipinos to get fit. But mostly watch-ing his out-of-shape friends trying to lose their prodigious bel-lies cracks him up.

And then there is the meteor tattoo on his left forearm. Pacquiao says his left punch is like a meteor that hits and explodes, sending his opponents to oblivion. He told his entourage that he would give $1,500 to everyone in the group who got a left-arm tattoo. Everyone started showing up with one. Pacquiao giggled every time he saw a new one.

The entourage has always been a funny story known among boxing insiders, but a few years ago it went global.

In April 2007, Home Box Office (HBO), which has 40 million subscribers in the United States, introduced the four-part documentary series *De La Hoya/Mayweather 24/7*. It was an inside look at Oscar De La Hoya and Floyd May-weather Jr., as they prepared for their junior middleweight title bout. It came on after *The Sopranos* and *Entourage*, two quality shows that drew millions of viewers. (*The Sopranos* had 7.7 million viewers, and *Entourage* had about 3.8 million, which were both considered hits in the cable television universe).

Ross Greenburg, the president of HBO Sports, had wanted to do a boxing reality show for a while. He had wanted to create the program around the June 2005 fight between Arturo Gatti and Floyd Mayweather, but higher-ups wanted to introduce it around a megafight. Enter De La Hoya versus Mayweather. "All the stars aligned," Greenburg told me. "We really had a blank slate; we weren't sure what we would come up with."

The show caught on instantly.

Showing the aging nature of its fans, demographers considered boxing aficionados as primarily a male thirty-five-plus group, but *24/7* brought in younger people. Forty-four percent of its viewers were eighteen to forty-nine, and executives started hearing from more and more young people that they loved the show, which could be accurately described as a sophisticated infomercial. Floyd Mayweather "jumped through the screen," says Greenburg, who had observed his children watching a lot of reality shows and wanted to replicate the genre for boxing. As the reality show craze hit its peak, *24/7* brought an inside look at real characters with extraordinary talents. A devastating loss can derail a fighter's career, and since most boxers come from nothing, there was a tension-filled natural story arc. "We wanted to get into the viewer's bloodstream," says Greenburg. Mayweather is a ham. De La Hoya, a typically more guarded person, let the cameras into his life. Thirty production personnel work on each edition of the program, and they shoot three hundred hours of footage. Both fighters were concerned about giving away too much training camp strategy, but the actual training footage was the least interesting. HBO did a brilliant job of developing characters: Mayweather's loose and sometimes strange behavior in his Las Vegas camp; De La Hoya acting like the classy veteran in Puerto Rico. Adding a story line, De La Hoya had fired Mayweather's uncle, Roger, as his trainer, and then he hired Freddie Roach. Roger Mayweather and Roach are long-standing rivals, and their tense relationship created a subplot going into the fight. The signature Jose Cancela musical score—*ba, ba, ba, bump, bump*—created drama in itself. It was the electronic age's answer to boxing's classic book, W. C. Heinz's *The Professional*. American media conglomerates had been ignoring boxing for years, but *24/7* did an end-around. The *New York Times* and *Time* magazine— which entitled one of its articles, "Will the De La Hoya– Mayweather Fight Save Boxing?"—covered the fight with gusto. Boxing wasn't exactly backed by the American mainstream, but it had entered the sports conversation again. The quality of the program and the interest it generated in the characters of boxing was so successful that HBO made *24/7* a part of its leadups to megafights. When Manny Pacquiao fought in 2008, an HBO crew started hanging around, giving a glimpse into Manny's world. "His colorful entourage adds a nice texture to a compelling personality," says Greenburg, who believes the greatest boxers have also been its best marketers (Ali, Leonard). Pacquiao also decided to start learning English a few months before his first appearance on the show, and his soft-spoken voice connected with Americans. Greenburg says Pacquiao is perfect for television because he is an always-evolving story: his political ambitions, his self-improvement goals, the mystery of him. "I have spent time with him, and he is enormously sincere. I don't think there is a bad bone in his body," says Greenburg. "He has a naiveté, an endearing innocence, a boyish charm; he is personable, and friendly . . . until he steps into the ring."

While HBO is not shown in every home, and Pacquiao's fights are usually pay-per-view affairs, the show helped create a renewed fascination with boxing. By 2010, 24/7 had become the most honored sports series on television in the previous three seasons with twelve sports Emmy Awards.

"We have accomplished our mission: launching stars, bringing a younger, hipper audience to the sport," says Greenburg. "24/7 has launched Mayweather and Pacquiao into the stratosphere. There would be no Mayweather and Pacquiao without 24/7. They are at a different level."

"THEY'RE ALL competing to be golden boy for the day," says Roach about Pacquiao's entourage. "Clean his pool. Take his shoes off. They will do anything for Manny Pacquiao." Roach laughs. The surrounding atmosphere instantly created likeability with the burgeoning star. Pacquiao might have been a Filipino from God-knows-where, but Middle Americans could relate to him almost more than any other fighter: He laughed a lot, he prided himself on hard work, he helped his impoverished people (HBO showed little Filipino girls screaming sweetly, "THANK

YOU, MAN-NY PAC-Q-UIAO"), and he talked about how he wanted to please the fans most of all. Having an entourage has become a given in professional sports. But Pacquiao's gang wasn't a reflection of an athlete with an outsized ego as much as a fun-loving and generous person.

Each episode of 24/7 spends about ten minutes with each fighter. There are many subtleties that are left on the cutting room floor and taboo subjects that are never really broached. The program is compelling, but it *was* created to promote a pay-per-view fight. While Pacquiao surrounds himself with jesters, and Americans are amused by his entourage, his group gets a different reaction in the Philippines where people live and breathe the Pacquiao soap opera.

Michael Koncz, a Canadian, is known as Pacquiao's closest adviser, or at least the one who is around the boss the most. He is the subject of a great deal of speculation. Roach introduced Koncz to Pacquiao. He says that Koncz was trying to get a fighter out of jail and went broke doing so. The incarcerated fighter went before a judge and expressed no remorse, then "told the judge he was going to kill her," according to Roach. Koncz was down on his luck, Roach says. "So Michael Koncz is hanging around the gym one day, and I introduce him to Manny Pacquiao. [Koncz] had a sob story— his wife left him and he had four kids he raised himself—and Manny Pacquiao felt sorry for him and gave him a job." There is a great deal of tension between Roach and Koncz. "I don't go through him. I go through Manny Pacquiao to negotiate my deal before every fight. You know, five minutes talking about it, we're done." I had heard around the gym that Koncz had a law degree and asked Roach about it. He replies with a laugh, "Bullshit. He was a gym hand at the Wild Card! Law degree!" While Roach and Koncz exchange greetings, they are hardly close. "Michael Koncz thinks Manny pays me too much money, and the thing is I introduced Michael Koncz to Manny Pacquiao. If it wasn't for me . . . if he didn't know me, he would have never met Manny Pacquiao, but he forgets that." The conditioning coach Alex Ariza and Koncz engaged in a fistfight, which took three people to pull Ariza off the Canadian. Koncz had wanted to be in the corner during a fight, and Ariza "bitch slapped" him. Ariza seems proud that he put Koncz in his place. Pacquiao admonished both men for creating chaos. An unidentified culprit hung a sign inside the gym. It reads, "The meeting for the Mike Koncz Fan Club has been canceled." Roach claims no knowledge of the sign's source, but his eyes sparkle when he reads it. Referring to Pacquiao, Roach adds: "I know this: Alex doesn't cut his meat for him. Mike Koncz does."

THE FREE-FOR-ALL at the Wild Card, which has become a place of boxing lore, has forced Roach to employ more restrictions on access to the gym. Roach ejected a man one day. "I put my hands on his shoulders and told him it was time to leave," Roach says. "There was no contact. I pointed him to the exit." Roach was sued. A Wild Card employee watched the man walk to the corner liquor store inside the same strip mall as the Wild Card on Vine Street, call 911, and then lie down on the street when he heard the sirens coming. The jury sided with Roach, dismissing every claim. "That guy's now banned from the Philippine community," Roach says.

Besides the provincial people in the entourage and the inside dramas with Pacquiao's closest boxing advisers (he has a whole other entourage in his political life), many people back in the Philippines don't understand why he lets some of the more dubious characters into his world.

LUIS "CHAVIT" SINGSON, a slight man who favors gaudy jewelry, is the kind of guy who has a pet tiger in his backyard ("He treats it like a house cat," someone told me), drives around a *tank proof* vehicle, and tells stories about how he was almost killed one night at a dance club when someone rolled two live hand grenades onto the dance floor; he saw the explosives and did what anyone in their right mind would have done: He hugged his girlfriend tight when the explosion hit. He was the only one who lived. "Luckily I was dancing with a fat woman at the time, and she took all the shrapnel," he says. ("One crazy bastard," a Filipino friend told me, laughing.)

Singson reached broader fame because he went public with a claim of paying off President Joseph Estrada. Estrada denied taking bribes. Estrada is a Filipino icon, a loveable rogue. It was an open secret that he drank too much, and in the presidential palace the staff would serve his Chivas Regal out of a teapot. And Estrada really liked drinking tea. He carried wads of cash, always tipping the military pilots who flew the presidential helicopter. Seriously normal behavior in the Philippines. Singson says that he personally delivered millions in illegal gambling money—US$200,000 every month—to the president inside the presidential palace. Singson's charges helped get Estrada thrown out of office:

Filipinos believed his claims because they don't tend to believe their presidents. Singson told journalists about the president's all-night drinking and million-dollar mahjong sessions, the need for the money to take care of his six mistresses and one official wife, and the deals for cronies in an explosive trial in 2000, which featured accusations and counter-accusations between Singson and the president. One witness, a retired general and former national police director, who testified that shortly after assuming office in 1998, Estrada had called him to the presidential palace for a meeting with the president and Singson. He said Estrada ordered him to work with Singson, who was assigned to coordinate an illegal, but tolerated, gambling operation called *jueteng*. Singson had made the same claim but said that he later broke with Estrada after the president gave a gambling franchise to one of Singson's rivals. As reported in the *New York Times*, Singson also claimed that Estrada tried to have him ambushed.

Singson is known to greet death threats and just about anything negative leveled against him, with the kind of naked aggression reserved for men who, when finding their common-law-wife in bed with a younger man, beat the man and woman senseless with a pipe. When this actually happened to Singson, he told the *Philippine Star*, "*Mabait pa nga ako, hindi ko sila pinatay* (I was still good, I did not kill them)." He has five children with the woman, Che. Then the former Ilocos Sur governor described the size of the penis of Che's lover as one for the books. "*Pinakamaliit na ari ang nakita ko, pang* Guinness Book of World Records (It was so tiny, it can qualify for the *Guinness Book of World Records*)," he remarked.

When HBO was in the Philippines and showed Pacquiao training there, there was concern for everyone's safety as a typhoon approached the archipelago. Roach wanted to get the hell out of there. In the documentary, Roach approaches Pacquiao, who sits with Singson, and implores him to leave. Pacquiao looks nervous for the first time ever, trying to tell Roach—with his eyes—to shut the hell up. ("If Michael Jordan was hanging around a guy like this, I'm sure it wouldn't be accepted," Roach says.)

People tell me, in a fond way, that Singson is one of the toughest sonsabitches in a notoriously violent country, but supposedly one heck of a nice guy in person. Not only does Singson go in the ring with Pacquiao, the two men enjoy marathon games of poker.

Michael Koncz concludes, "If you're a friend of Manny, you're his friend."

Singson has been called the Filipino Al Pacino. And Pacquiao likes to identify himself as a gangster type. In one of his most beloved photographs, which was set up in a Hollywood studio, Pacquiao wears a pinstripe suit and puffs on a cigar, resembling Pacino's Tony Montana character in *Scarface*.

It is the Filipino paradox: overt kindness and overt violence.

Pacquiao comes from a warrior culture, and he embraces many different figures. Controlling others' actions is not really possible, but given Pacquiao's fame, people close to him are also in the public spotlight.

In the summer of 2010, police raided the home of Pacquiao's elder sister, Isidra Paglinawan, in an anti-gambling crackdown. Pacquiao has publicly denied allegations that his siblings have illegal gambling operations. After the raid, Pacquiao told police, "I will not interfere. Let the law take its course." Pacquiao has never been directly connected with any illegal gambling operations, but his willingness to embrace everyone worries some of his handlers, who don't want him to spoil his image or get him beheaded or something. There seems to be a great deal of naïveté swirling around. Pacquiao doesn't seem to realize that the underground figures want to be around him because *he* is a pure national hero.

ONE DAY, at the Wild Card, Robert Duvall, who played Tom Hagen, a consigliore, in *The Godfather*, came into the gym. Pacquiao's mouth guard was easily visible because his smile was so wide. He has a DVD collection of *The Godfather* series. Pacquiao also collects guns. In the Philippines, he sometimes carries a pistol. A gym hand brought a bar stool for Duvall, who doesn't get around so well anymore, so he could watch the workout. Duvall's assistant, a handsome Filipino, translated for him. Duvall absolutely loved being in the place, and the Filipino television crews were suddenly overjoyed because they had a story for their producers back in Manila. They lay in wait to interview the actor. Somehow they knew that Duvall had been to the Philippines many years ago, and the reporters asked him his impressions of their native land. This is a deadly trap because Filipinos are so hospitable that any sign of disrespect will bring the longest faces you'll ever see: "Everybody is *this tall* and their national sport is . . . *basketball*!" quipped the actor. The Filipinos thought the line was hilarious, and Duvall went on to say how much he *loved* Filipinos. The journalists were melting into the Wild Card's sweat-drenched floor. Roach really likes having celebrities around. He gets a kick out of them. But all the commotion can kind of get on his nerves, too. He is, after all, trying to train a world-class fighter to prevail—and not be killed.

As Pacquiao went through his workout, Roach shook a bit more than normal. ("It amazes me that he is the same guy that walked in the first day," says Roach. "His work ethic is exactly the same. Guys get comfortable; guys get lazy after winning a world title. Guys get cocky. He hasn't. He trains his ass off everyday. He has many distractions outside the ring, a lot of chaos, a lot of drama, but he can separate that. Whatever else is going on in his life, he leaves it outside.") There were almost two-dozen spectators, and now it made Roach uneasy. *Are they spies?* Roach who gains good intel from reporters and other sorts of characters coming into his gym had heard that a Pacquiao sparring partner had been blabbing to a competitor. Roach, antsy, didn't like it one bit. After observing a sparring session and then having a bunch of photographs taken, Duvall finally decided to leave. He sat next to me, and I encouraged him to stay and watch Pacquiao shadowbox.

DUVALL STUCK AROUND. He sat on the grey bench close to the apron. It was suddenly obvious to everybody in the Wild Card that something quite special must be going on inside Manny Pacquiao because there was so much angry beauty coming out. He was dancing now, the speed and flowing grace of his feet, punctuated by his fists, like lasers, precisely cutting through the air. He was playing make-believe;

pretending his opponent was across from him, he would look, eyes narrowing at his own image in the mirror, checking his form, sliding around the ring as if he were on air, pirouetting, and throwing combinations. He went on for something like ten minutes. He seemed transformed.

Duvall was silent, looking almost overwhelmed. At the end, he said a quiet thank you, and departed.

6

THE PROMOTERS

ONE O'CLOCK on a Wednesday in Hollywood. Journalists and a lot of freak show boxing geeks playing pretend journalists stand in the Wild Card's parking lot. There was a time—before pay-per-view and the Internet—when writers from major metropolitan papers covered the various intrigues in boxing and had firsthand knowledge of the fight game. ("There are no fighters that the general public is fascinated by that have charisma, that transcend their sport," says Tom Jolly, the *New York Times* sports editor who, when he said that in 2009, had attended only one prize fight.) The small fraternity of legitimate Filipino, Mexican and part-time American journalists are standing on the warm pavement—all waiting for a chance to interview Pacquiao and his handlers. Outnumbering the legitimate reporters is a freak show—bloggers, collectible hunters, autograph vermin, and a Pacquiao impersonator who has a fake mustache and puts shoes on his knees to look short for his "Minny Pacquiao" Web show. We're trying to elbow past the imposters so we can interview Pacquiao and his promoter, Bob Arum. The chatter is once again about American Floyd Mayweather Jr., considered the second best pound-for-pound boxer in the world and a fighter who was on the show *Dancing with the Stars*—whose camp has been talking about how (and this is not made up) Filipinos have some sort of special powers against pain and can even withstand bullets. A hundred of us, including me, descend upon Arum, Manny Pacquiao's Brooklyn-born, Harvard-educated promoter. He came into the boxer's life about two-thirds of the way through the Filipino's career. He is basking in the scrum's attention. Arum, seventy-nine, is a legend. Allen Grubman, "the king of music entertainment law" and a friend of Arum's, says that his clients, including Bruce Springsteen, Bono, and Elton John, want to meet Arum. He promoted Muhammad Ali, and he helps steer the course of modern boxing. Not surprisingly, he has a few stories to tell and is willing to say anything to draw attention to one of his promotions. He has a low roar to his voice—scratchy and boosterish:

"Mayweather's talking about Filipinos taking drugs that can fend off bullets. He is saying that five hundred years ago they took a pill and bullets can't penetrate them, and so—I don't know—Mayweather is crazy."

"Does Pacquiao want to fight Mayweather?" someone shouts.

"Yeah, he would like to fight Mayweather, but no one is going to bully a Filipino. [Sage nods from the Filipinos.] Floyd Mayweather is a coward."

Arum has been upset with Mayweather. He is in a war with Mayweather's promoter, Oscar De La Hoya and wants to create controversy. He is a hell of a fun guy to listen to because he is strikingly intelligent, funny, opinionated, and crude.

And right there it dawns on me that everything about the modern boxing game is confined to this chaotic parking lot at the foot of the Wild Card Gym. And now boxing has Manny Pacquiao, the greatest boxer to come along since Muhammad Ali, and all that people want to talk about is . . . Floyd Mayweather *and* a fight that looks unlikely to ever happen.

WEARING A tailored jacket and a turtleneck, Arum cuts a rather elegant figure among the rabble. "A brilliant man," someone says. I ask a blogger for an impression: "A fucking genius." Arum is the ruddy-faced president of Top Rank and negotiates the champ's deals and takes a healthy cut of them. In his four-decade career, Arum has been around many of the greats, including Ali and Leonard, two stars that are American icons. Arum's ability to have Manny Pacquiao under contract means he is one of the most powerful figures in boxing. He believes Pacquiao has the goods to transcend the sport.

Arum cut his teeth in the Justice Department in the Southern District of New York, heading the taxation group that held up the purse of the first Floyd Patterson-Sonny Liston fight, because of reported illegalities by one of the promoters, Roy Cohn. It was 1965. Arum wore horned-rimmed glasses and was a skinny, Harvard graduate. Sonny Liston came to Arum's office because he was owed about $160,000 for the fight and Liston says to him, "Where's my money?"

Arum says, "I'm an assistant United States attorney. Behave yourself."

Despite an early aversion to boxing ("two guys clubbing each other over the head"), Arum grew to love the sport.

Equally thoughtful and humorously crass, Arum tends to expound on a variety of subjects, from religion to history, in a style that could be described as rhetorical grandstanding. He's had some terrific promotions, including the second Ali-Frazier fight, the Hagler-Hearns fight, the first Leonard-Duran fight, and several others that he did with Muhammad Ali. He has had a few run-ins with boxing commissions, and the FBI has turned over his offices at least once. About the encroachment of mixed martial arts fighting on the popularity of boxing, Arum says, in his Brooklyn accent, "For me, I look at the UFC audience and the boxing audience as being two different audiences entirely. Our audience in boxing is ethnic: Hispanic, Filipino, Puerto Rican, Mexican, and the hardcore boxing fan that can't watch . . . like me . . . can't watch UFC. UFC are a bunch of skinhead white guys watching people in the ring who also look like skinhead white guys. For me, and people like me, it is not something they ever care to see. They've watched it. It's horrible. Guys rolling around like homosexuals on the ground." Then a few months later I am asking him about an upcoming fight, and he enthusiastically tells me that Dana White, the most influential person in mixed martial arts as the president of the UFC, is coming to one of his promotions. "White is talking up the fight," says Arum, happily. "He's doing something called Twittering—ever heard of that?" When reminded about his derogatory comments about the UFC, he laughs them off. "That was just my personal feeling about the sport."

Arum's world is a derivative of *Raging Bull*. Don King, his rival of four decades, calls him "Lonesome Bob" and once called him a rat fink for testifying for the government in a bribery trial. "He's going to try to make himself a hero for being a rat fink," King said in 2000 after Arum admitted during a federal trial that he paid the International Boxing Federation (IBF) president a bribe in order to gain a more favorable rating for one of his fighters. "You can't be no hero being a rat fink," King continued. "You know how you be the hero? Don't participate in rat fink-ism." The Nevada Athletic Commission penalized Arum and fined him $125,000 for offering the payoff. "Lessons can be learned, not only by us, but by the commission and everyone in boxing," Arum said.

ONCE, WHEN CHIDED by a reporter about conflicting statements he had made on successive days, Arum said, "I was lying yesterday; today I'm telling the truth."

Promoters, for better or worse, shape the sport of boxing. They build careers by supporting fighters early on and try and build them into box office stars. They are also criticized, sometimes wrongly, for destroying the sport because there are so many ficfdoms and rabid self-interest that the best fights are not always made. Boxing is full of mysterious confrontations. Didn't-you-just-call-that-guy-a-motherfucker? And-now-you're . . . *hugging him*?

Every fight promoter wants Manny Pacquiao, the sport's biggest star. Arum has had to wage his own war to keep him from joining Oscar De La Hoya's Golden Boy Promotions, a significant force in boxing.

De La Hoya, the charming and intelligent Mexican American boxer, was once extremely close with Arum. At Arum's sixty-fifth birthday party at a Reno hotel ballroom, De La Hoya presented his prized Olympic gold medal to the promoter. "It was a stunner, it made the night, and Bob was very emotional," says Bill Caplan, Top Rank's longtime publicist, recalling the 1996 party.

The De La Hoya–Arum union originated in the afterglow of the 1992 Barcelona Olympic Games at which the fighter won his gold medal. Arum had spent the previous decade promoting middleweight Marvin Hagler's super bouts and was in the midst of the successful George Foreman comeback. But he saw something special in De La Hoya. NBC's Olympics coverage had focused on the boxer's promise to his dying mother that he would win the gold medal for her. The good son also was a good-looking, power-punching American hero who spoke fluent Spanish and held great appeal in the emerging Latino market, a burgeoning market that Arum was determined to build his company around.

After Barcelona, the Golden Boy easily dispatched a succession of obscure professional opponents and over-the-hill foes like Julio Cesar Chavez. To exploit De La Hoya's good looks, Arum planted news conference crowds with attractive women holding up "Marry me, Oscar" signs. The first small rift in the boxer-promoter relationship was seen in early 1999, when De La Hoya told a Spanish-language television station at a Dodger Stadium news conference that he had threatened to leave Arum if the promoter agreed to a rematch clause with world-class opponent Ike Quartey. The storm passed when Arum designated De La Hoya a co-promoter of the victory over Quartey.

"It was a big misinterpretation," De La Hoya said afterward. "I will be happy with Bob Arum for the rest of my career. He's the reason I'm here."

Meanwhile, Arum continued to enrich the partnership: He created an extremely lucrative fight with Felix Trinidad in 1999, which set records for the richest non-heavyweight fight in history. De La Hoya dominated Trinidad in the early rounds but became more defensive as the fight went on. The Golden Boy lost the fight and tarnished his perfect record. Then De La Hoya learned that Arum had earned $12 million from the fight. The promoter's share was a staggering sum, and De La Hoya harbored deep resentment, despite the fact that his own take totaled $23 million. "We made a lot of money together," De La Hoya told the *Los Angeles Times*, but he couldn't get over his feeling that Arum also deprived him of "millions and millions of dollars." Arum would manage De La Hoya's career to earnings estimated at $225 million.

Not long afterward, he started Golden Boy Promotions. De La Hoya, who holds a high school equivalency degree, fired everyone around him and hired Swiss banker Richard Schaefer to run his company. Schaefer and Arum have been feuding, on and off, ever since. De La Hoya lost a June 2000 decision to Sugar Shane Mosley, and he railed in the post-fight news conference that perhaps Arum had something to do with the scoring that also triggered a rematch clause. In August 2000 the men went to federal court. De La Hoya filed suit to terminate his partnership with Arum. After a federal judge granted the boxer's request for summary judgment, making the former champion's contract with Arum null and void, De La Hoya said he had just "defeated one of the biggest Jews to come out of Harvard."

Being the two biggest promoters in boxing, they inevitably have to work together because each company has many of the best fighters in their stables so they have to co-promote events. De La Hoya went against Fernando Vargas, Mosley (again), and Bernard Hopkins, to whom De La Hoya lost in a ninth-round knockout. Right after the fight, De La Hoya signed Hopkins and announced that Golden Boy would promote both Hopkins's and De La Hoya's fights. Arum went nuts and told reporters that De La Hoya had "quit" in the Hopkins bout, which is about the worst thing you can say about a fighter. Also chapping Arum was Golden Boy's success at signing name fighters, like Mosley, Marco Antonio Barrera, Winky Wright, and Juan Manuel Marquez.

All of this acrimony came to a head over Manny Pacquiao.

In September 2006 De La Hoya tried to steal the Filipino away from Top Rank. De La Hoya approached Freddie Roach about meeting Pacquiao. Roach facilitated the meeting because he felt Pacquiao should listen to offers, like any other athlete. They all rode in a limo (there was a briefcase next to De La Hoya), but Roach decided to leave the vehicle. Knowing Pacquiao's predilection for cash, De La Hoya had $250,000 in the briefcase. They went to the Beverly Hills steakhouse, Morton's. Pacquiao, who struggles to say no when cash is involved, signed a seven-fight contract with Golden Boy. Bob Arum was livid. Richard Schaefer—the president of Golden Boy—and De La Hoya met with Pacquiao at Morton's Steakhouse but would not admit to any cash exchange. He said the form of payment to Pacquiao was irrelevant. Pacquiao received at least one check as a bonus payment, Schaefer said.

Then, in November, Arum counterattacked. He gave Pacquiao a $1 million bonus and claimed the Golden Boy contract was invalid. Amid dueling lawsuits, Pacquiao continued with Arum.

Pacquiao seems to regret his betrayal, but he has a difficult time saying no. He also has a great deal of respect for De La Hoya, one of the few boxers to have such enormous success in the business world.

Through the last five years, Arum and Pacquiao have become close friends. Arum has traveled to the Philippines to support Pacquiao's political career. But their relationship is complicated, and money is at the center of it. Pacquiao has reportedly taken advances from Top Rank to help pay for his political campaigning and lifestyle. Pacquiao sends his children to an international school outside of Manila. He sponsors nine-ball billiard games in which the Philippines' best players compete, which has a pot of one million pesos. His trio of American co-managers receives 20 percent of his purse, while Freddie Roach earns 10 percent. A chunk also goes to the U.S. Internal Revenue Service (IRS) for taxes, and another chunk is for promotional fees at Top Rank. Pacquiao spends hundreds of thousands of dollars of his own money for tickets. He has to maintain a fleet of vehicles, a handful of condos, apartments, and houses, and pay the freeloaders, and give his money to the poor. Pacquiao's spending habits, it is argued, have been good for Top Rank because Pacquiao must continue boxing to earn even more money.

In the summer of 2007, Arum and De La Hoya declared a truce. Arum said he would give back De La Hoya's 1992 Olympic gold medal. They would stop battling over the promotional rights, and they would co-promote a fight between Pacquiao and Marco Antonio Barrera, a Golden Boy fighter.

"The biggest winner in this is the fans," Golden Boy Chief Executive Richard Schaefer said. "The biggest and best fights in boxing can now happen."

"Once the mediator broke our logjam [over Pacquiao], the animosity just melted away," said Arum. "It had a cathartic effect, where you rid yourself of any bad feelings you've harbored for years."

The good will didn't last. Since 2007, the thaw has slowly turned into a deep freeze. The personal animosity between Arum and De La Hoya means the most anticipated fight in twenty years—Pacquiao versus Floyd Mayweather Jr.—has suffered countless delays. And there is another twist: Arum once represented Mayweather.

FROM 1996 UNTIL 2006, Top Rank promoted Floyd Mayweather Jr. Now Mayweather accuses Arum of underpaying him, exploiting his talents, and manipulating officials. "You wouldn't let me be," Mayweather says about their decade-long partnership. At a journalist's forum a few years ago, Mayweather went off on Uncle Bob, "Cut the middle man out, and see what you can get. You were talking about paying me two or three million when it really should have been six million. And once I cut the middle man out, it became fifteen or thirty million." Don King was there. Arum and King had been dueling, in and out of court, for four decades, but Mayweather was attacking the grand tradition of boxing promotion. The dispute highlights the unenlightened self-interest of the sport.

"I am not a defender of Bob Arum, though I am a defender of the sport," King said. Nodding toward Arum, King said, "Oscar De La Hoya would never be where he is today without this man right here. This man has been a foe to me all these years. But that's what makes me so good. I wouldn't know how good I am if I didn't have a Bob Arum. I think Floyd is great, but he doesn't understand. You have to crawl before you walk and walk before you run." He said that though Mayweather was correct about how much money he'd made in his last two fights, Mayweather conveniently ignored the work that Arum did in building his career and guiding him to the pinnacle. "Floyd Mayweather would not be getting the money he's getting from Oscar De La Hoya without Bob Arum," King said, as Mayweather tried to speak over him. "You're going to make a lot of money in your career. I just want you to understand the principles involved. Someone has to make a person big. You're not born big. I understand what you're saying, Floyd. But you also have to understand how you got to where you are so you could go and make all this money. Remember him."

"You know me," King said—to the journalist Kevin Iole—doing six things at once as his throng of assistants slowly ushered him toward an elevator. "Truth, justice, and the American way. It ain't right what the kid said. I knew that, and I had to say something."

King was saying that promoters take chances on a lot of fighters and invest in their careers. Boxers don't always realize the behind-the-scenes expenses. Like many boxers, Pacquiao has had to go through his share of promoter problems. In April 2005, he filed suit against Murad Muhammad in federal court in New York, claiming that Muhammad joined with Pacquiao's business managers to divert 30 percent of his purses to a dummy company that was supposed to pay Pacquiao's U.S. income taxes but never did. According to the suit, "Muhammad had facilitated a scheme that permitted Pacquiao's business managers to retain as much as 50 percent or more of Pacquiao's earnings." This was a painful issue for Pacquiao because his business managers were Rod Nazario and Rod Rudolfo Nazario. Nazario had brought him to the United States. The promoter had cared for him. He was practically family. Complicating matters, Pacquiao attorney Keith Davidson said the Internal Revenue Service wanted to withhold Pacquiao's entire $1.75 million purse before the Morales fight. However, after negotiations with Davidson and co-managers Nick Khan and Shelly Finkel, the IRS decided to withhold just 30 percent of the gross purse, or $525,000, Davidson said. "So [Pacquiao] picked people he thought he could trust to do the right thing for him," Davidson told the Las Vegas Review Journal. "Manny wanted to do the right thing all the time. When we met with the IRS people, and they saw how egregiously Manny had been treated, I think they understood what we as his new management team were trying to do." Federal law requires promoters to withhold 30 percent of the purses of nonresident aliens. An agent from the local IRS office frequently attends the news conferences of fights in Las Vegas in which foreigners are participating in an effort to make certain the proper amount of tax is withheld. In a statement released by David-son, Pacquiao said, "It has taken me a while to come to terms with the fact that I have been cheated by people whom I trusted. I intend to see this suit to the bitter end so that I can recover every dollar that was stolen from me, as well as help protect other fighters from being taken advantage of by Mr. Muhammad.

"As for the immediate future, my fans can rest assured that I will be fighting soon, but not with Murad Muhammad or M&M Sports as my promoter. As of today, I have instructed my new management to begin negotiating for my next fight and fights thereafter. I will never fight again for Murad Muhammad and M&M Sports."

A settlement was reached just as the jury went into deliberations to reach a verdict in the trial at federal court in Manhattan, reported the *New York Daily News.* Pacquiao got an undisclosed amount of money and was freed from his promotional contract with Muhammad. In press reports, Muhammad said, "We will go on with our lives. We will find another Pacquiao, or even better. I will continue to build another Pacquiao, continue to help Fil-ipino boxers and all Asian boxers if they want my help. I wish Manny all the luck. I feel he should go on to be as suc-cessful as he can and represent the Philippines with honor. May God be with him."

Over the past few years, Pacquiao has bounced from Murad Muhammad to Gary Shaw to Shelly Finkel to Bob Arum's Top Rank. His career, though, will be defined by Arum, who makes the fights and helps to create the Pac-Man's image.

IT WAS A JUNE EVENING in New York. Hot and humid, it felt like a *shvitz*. The boxing world was at the Friar's Club—a faux Tudor building on East 55th Street. It is a place in which rooms are named after classic American entertainers, such as George Burns and Ed Sullivan, and there are photos of Frank Sinatra, Buddy Hackett, and Phyllis Diller on the walls. Bob Arum, "longtime Friar," was being honored in what was billed as a tribute, but many people had decided it had to be a roast. Arum was just too controversial of a character (think: George Steinbrenner) to give sincere speeches about. There were so many people who wanted to come that they had to rent a room at the Hilton a few blocks away because the Friar's Club couldn't accommodate the four-hundred-plus crowd. The evening would be about Bob Arum, and the people who knew him best would roast him. The event was an unplugged peek inside Arum and the world of boxing promotion. It inevitably came back to Manny Pacquiao.

Arum sat in a leather chair on the stage. Jim Lampley, HBO's boxing commentator, who has become the voice of the sport, was slated as the master of ceremonies.

Fred Roman, the president of the Friar's Club, said: "Boxing is a great sport. It was such a thrill for me as a young comedian at the start of my career to watch Rocky Marciano train in the Catskills. Fighter after fighter trained in the Catskill Mountains and still won bouts—*even after eating chopped liver.* It's hard to believe."

Sitting in their coats and ties was a who's who of boxing: Thomas Hearns, George Foreman, Ray "Boom Boom" Mancini, and Manny Pacquiao. Roman talked about how

Arum had promoted Muhammad Ali. A cell phone went off. "Is that a phone? If it's my mother, tell her I wore a sweater. She worries."

Then the theme from *Rocky* began playing, and Roman introduced, "Kid Prune Juice!"

It was Mickey Freeman, a five foot three comedian who played Private Zimmerman on *Sergeant Bilko* for six years. Freeman was dressed as a fighter. Two scantily clad women stared in a comely way.

"My manager came up to me and said we're going to try something different in this round, 'When he hits you, hit him back.' I thought I would invite these broads," he said about the young women, suggesting an eventual liaison.

"That would be an assault with a dead weapon," replied Roman.

"I want Prune Juice!" George Foreman stormed into the room, as everyone laughed. Foreman said a few words, followed by Alan Grubman, Arum's rock 'n' roll manager friend, then Ray Mancini, the great lightweight champion who told an emotional story about how Arum had helped him get a title shot: "I wanted to win the title for my father, who I thought was unjustly denied the opportunity because of World War II." Mancini talked about how he got a title shot against Alexis Arguello, but he lost. Arum eventually gave Mancini another chance, and he won the title. "Other than seeing my children born, it was the greatest day of my life." He talked about Arum coming to Youngstown, Ohio, to present him with the championship belt, and Mancinci turned around and gave it to his father. "I will always appreciate that you gave me that opportunity."

After some remarks from Arum's son—a professor at New York University (NYU)—Stuie Stone, a comedian, came to the podium.

"Thank you, Jim. That was one of the most thrilling MC jobs ever. Listen, I am an insomniac, I have trouble sleeping, so could you call me on the phone later? How can I put this very delicately: You're a boring motherfucker. I want to thank Bob Arum for producing the longest night of my life. I sat in the dining room for an hour and a half, I couldn't get a main dish, and all the waiters were waiting for Manny Pacquiao. He didn't show up, they didn't care." In the grand tradition of the Friar's Club, Stone made some remarks, such as "Fuck you, Bob Arum!" and "If Don King were here, we would have three people in the room, because Don King fucked more black men than Little Richard." Stone concluded his remarks by saying, "This is a great night, to have four hundred people show up, and we don't even know who the fuck you are. We're honoring Bob Arum. Who the fuck is Bob Arum?"

After Stone, a movie, *The Marijuana Affair*, was shown. Arum had starred in it. Arum, the only white guy in the C-list film, looked down at Pacquiao, "Manny, I think it's almost as good as your pictures, right?"

Lou DiBella, a promoter, talked about his experiences with Arum: "I graduated from Harvard Law School, I worked at this big Wall Street law firm, and I got what I thought was my dream job to make the fights and work as a lawyer for HBO sports. We were in a room—a bunch of HBO executives and Bob—we were discussing a George Foreman fight. George was going to fight against a guy, "Cowboy" Jimmy Ellis. I said, 'Bob, this guy can barely stand up.' If you know Bob, there is a look that he gets right before he explodes, and his body contorts; it's like a cross between Joe Cocker and a constipated guy. And then he explodes, 'Kid, you're two fucking weeks out of law school, and you don't know shit. Shut the fuck up.' I wanted to thank you for that moment. I didn't know shit, and you taught me that this was a vile and base enough business that I could actually be a success." The crowd laughed knowingly. "It was an important moment for me. He is the greatest promoter of the last half century. He can be so fucking mean, it is unbelievable. I don't know how many times he had me shaking because he was so fucking miserable to me. He has a heart. Genaro Hernandez, a mutual friend who he promoted, a former world champion, he was diagnosed with a horrible cancer that figured to kill him in a matter of a couple of months. The only thing that would save him was a treatment that wouldn't be covered by any insurance; it would be incredibly costly. Genaro is alive today because of Bob Arum. May you have many more years of acting like a prick but being a nicer guy than anyone knows."

Then Todd duBoef, his stepson, who works at Top Rank:

"I was twenty-six; I was to learn from a master, an icon in sports, a childhood's dream. The William Morris mailroom couldn't compare; I was going to learn patience, professionalism, integrity, and relationships. But he gave me rule number one, [Brooklyn accent] 'Don't ever fall in love with a fighta'; they'll break your heart.'

"First course: network relations. He was the Sheik, I was the shadow. We headed for 6th Avenue, and off we went to a beautiful wood boardroom, said our pleasantries; we sat down, and in three minutes they were "fucking morons" who didn't know shit about this sport. He berated the *fucking buyer*! We were escorted out of the building in a nice fashion; they could see the meeting didn't go well.

"We got in the car, and he got on his cell phone and called everybody in the media and told them just what he thought about those executives on 6th Avenue. We hurried to JFK for a flight back to Las Vegas. Flight delay. Corner of my eye, I see the master, suitcase above his head. He throws the suitcase against the wall of the terminal. What did I get myself into?

"Next day I show up in the office. The press clips were coming in. 'Arum Bashes Network Executives.' I shuddered. I peaked into his office. There was a sparkle in his eyes, a grin from ear-to-ear. [Brooklyn accent] 'Hey, did you see the press? Sensational, huh?'

"My education was in full swing.

"This started the whole birth of the fuck 'em philosophy.

"What this philosophy did was change the sport, it changed media; he took it from terrestrial television to closed circuit to premium cable to where we are today to see it on pay-per-view.

"But more importantly, what he did was planted a seed. He planted a seed to all of those young kids who came out of poverty, out of humble, humble beginnings, from the Olympics to pro debuts, and gave them an opportunity to be relevant, to be world figures.

"Tonight, this is my lesson to you, and this lesson is a special one.

"It was last November, and it was the Manny Pacquiao–Miguel Cotto fight. It was Sunday, and the results looked sensational. It was chilling. Bob, we are going to do fantastic. We have done a great job. There was silence. Bob, what's wrong? [Brooklyn accent] 'I've got a pit in my stomach.' You've got a pit in your stomach; this is one of the great. . . . 'I don't want to see one of the guys lose. This reminds me of Tommy and Marvin.'" DuBoef was choking up. "Well, Bob, you broke rule number one; you always fell in love with the fighters."

Ross Greenberg, president of HBO Sports, also gave a tribute.

"As you all know, Bob Arum is a very religious man, and he often takes trips to Jerusalem to visit the mountaintop where Moses roamed and talked to God. . . .

"God said one day, 'Bob, you must follow the Ten Commandments.'

"And Bob said, 'How about we negotiate a little bit. How's eight out of ten, and we will take out the ones on lying and cheating.'"

Manny Pacquiao, who many people had come to see, loved the evening. He was visiting New York with his wife and kids. He told the crowd, "I want to congratulate you on being a visionary promoter. I wasn't born when you started out in boxing. I was born, lately. Without you I can't make my dreams come true. So thanks to God and you."

THE SHAPING OF a fighter, from who he will fight to how he is sold to the public, is left to the promoter. Arum couldn't take all the credit. There had been others who had built Pacquiao through the years. But Arum had promoted his largest fights in the last five years. He took him from a boxing sensation to a larger star by helping to get the best matchups, sold his story to the media, and brokered his deals. The sport of boxing has always been under the auspices of competing promoters and has no central authority. The different factions, many of which work against each other, don't have a larger perspective, like the titans running the NFL or the NBA. Arum, in his waning years, wanted to make Pacquiao into a mainstream star. He wanted to sell boxing through Manny Pacquiao, who was a man of humility and charisma. He tended to overstate his case about Pacquiao being greater than Ali. In his heyday, Muhammad Ali, the icon, was fighting a war on many fronts—racism and the Vietnam War. *I ain't got no quarrel with them Vietcong.* The world is not divided over Manny Pacquiao. Ali was both loved and hated. Pacquiao doesn't engender those kinds of passions. Ali was also the heavyweight champion of the world—a bigger media platform—who fought in the last great heavyweight era. He, of course, had epic battles with fighters of his generation (Joe Frazier, Ken Norton), the previous generation (Sonny Liston), and the younger generation (George Foreman). "Ali became bigger than boxing," says José A. Sánchez Fournier, of *El Nuevo Día*. "Pacquiao is a similar figure. Not only has he become a mainstream figure in the United States and abroad, but he has become a true icon, representing more than his sport, or his country." And yet, by early 2010, Pacquiao had yet to fully reach anything near the status of an Ali. But there was no other athlete of his stature so poised to make a political impact. No one was sure if Arum truly believed that Pacquiao represented something more profound to the world or if that was just promoter-speak to get his client attention. It was too early in

Pacquiao's life. And yet, Pacquiao, if he became a congressman and someday even the president of the Philippines (hardly a far-fetched idea), well, perhaps Arum's boosterism would come to fruition. Arum helped shape Pacquiao's career and enriched Pacquiao. He helped pay for his political campaigns and, scary as it might seem, Bob Arum wielded a lot of influence in the future of almost 92 million Filipinos.

JIM LAMPLEY wound down the Arum roast by talking about Pacquiao as a crowd of Filipinos gathered outside to get a peek of their boxing hero. "Four things have to happen for someone to become a superstar like Manny Pacquiao. He has to win almost all of his fights, he has to be very exciting when he fights, he has to have a story to tell, and he has to have someone tell the story. In this case, all four of those elements came together, magically, perfectly, into what has become a global phenomenon. It's amazing to see what happened to Manny, and so much of that goes to Bob and his extraordinary skill and his vision."

Arum, a sentimentalist when he is not telling someone to fuck off, seemed touched by the evening:

"I graduated from the greatest law school in the world and served as an attorney in the Department of Justice. I never thought I would spend my life promoting a sport, let alone boxing, but it happened because Jim Brown, the great football player, introduced me to Muhammad Ali, and I was given the opportunity to promote a Muhammad Ali fight, and it was supposed to be against Ernie Terrell in Chicago, and the promotion was going great, and that's when Ali said, 'I ain't got no quarrel with them Viet Cong.' Mayor Daley threw us out of Chicago, and Ali got thrown out of the country. That's how it started. I had no experience. But having gone through that trial by fire, everything that happened in the last forty-four years was like a piece of cake. Nothing was as hard as that because . . . in that year . . . 1965, 1966, the Vietnam War was not popular, so when I came down on Ali's side, I was called a pariah and a lot worse. And it ended up that this guy with a heart of gold, Muhammad Ali, was right, and all of the other pundits were wrong. History proved him to be right so years later he stood and lit the Olympic torch in the presence of President Clinton. And that was a vindication that taught me, 'Stand up for what you believe.' If that means blowing a deal with a network, if it means really not advancing your business, you gotta do what you believe. My career mirrors what was going on in the United States and in the world. I started when the Black Power movement was just getting started. I was designated by Elijah Muhammad to be Muhammad Ali's manager and promoter. It's hard to remember, when there is a man of color in the White House, what this country was like back in the sixties. People fought so hard for recognition, and I played a small part in that. It really changed my life. Then as the years went on, I realized that this country was changing dramatically. Particularly when I moved to the Western part of the United States. That there were so many people who spoke Spanish who lived and worked in this country. And by the end of this century, 25 percent of all Americans will be of Hispanic heritage. We took that fact, and we devoted ourselves to promoting

Hispanic boxers. Great for these Hispanic kids, and great for our company. And the world is changing. Look at Manny Pacquiao. He comes from a country of 90 million people. Eleven million Filipinos work outside their country, with about 5 million living in the United States. These Filipinos have been dedicated to him, have followed him. It wasn't me, Manny. It was your fellow Filipinos, waiting outside, getting your autograph, buying tickets, letting us know what you are, who you are, and brought you the international fan base that you now have."

And the evening ended as the audience rushed to Manny Pacquiao.

7

DON'T QUOTE ME ON THE WOMEN

MANNY PACQUIAO HAS BECOME a subject of tabloid fodder in his homeland. His every move is the subject for idol gossipers, newspaper writers, supermarket rags, glossy magazines, and even the more traditional nightly news. If one scans Filipino newspapers to learn about the boxer, stories about his indiscretions inevitably appear. Are the innuendos and reports true or not? That is beside the point because they have become part of the dialogue around the public figure named Manny Pacquiao.

Pacquiao is married to Jinkee, who everyone describes as a kind person. She is attractive. Many Filipinos pride themselves on thinking they are color-blind, but they routinely wonder if she has some Caucasian heritage. She is known to surprise people with packages of General Santos delicacies. She has had to live out her life in public and must endure the prying eyes of millions. I have seen her leaving places—a church, a hotel—and hundreds of Filipinos, mostly older women, scream her name and want a photograph with her. For some, she is a representative of the status of Pinays, a put-upon group if there ever was one. Manny and Jinkee met when he was a twenty-year-old fighter and she was a beauty consultant at a GenSan mall.

They have been married for ten years. As her husband has become more famous, the spotlight has intensified on the couple, and their relationship has become tabloid fodder. Jinkee gives "exclusive interviews" in magazines like *StarStudio*, *Yes!*, and *People Asia*, and Jinkee and Manny's every gesture get dissected on national news broadcasts. In one issue of *StarStudio*, Jinkee addressed her husband's alleged extramarital affairs. The three names that Jinkee brought up in connection with her husband were Ara Mina, Valerie Concepcion, and Krista Ranillo. (Everyone involved denies the rumors.) About Ranillo, Jinkee was quoted in the story saying, "There are so many single men out there, right? Why does she need one who is married?" ABS-CBN News—a major news outlet—re-reports the more down-market journalism and also does some Pacquiao stories of its own. In December 2009, it produced a piece about Manny giving a diamond-encrusted ring to his wife as a "peace offering" after "the couple had several public tiffs due to rumors about the boxer's alleged affair with actress Krista Ranillo." (Manny has denied the affair.)

When Pacquiao was making his movie *Wapakman*, the Filipino papers started reporting the alleged tryst with Ranillo, a twenty-five-year-old *Maxim* cover girl. (When I was in the Philippines, women would ask me constantly, with a gossipy glee, if I had heard about the "Krista affair.") Filipino news broadcasts showed Jinkee crying during a Thanksgiving mass. On a tabloid TV show called *The Buzz*, a Filipina actress was quoted saying that "Krista Ranillo is not worth it." Then several months later the *Philippine Star* noted that Krista Ranillo was in Los Angeles while Pacquiao trained for his 2010 fight against Joshua Clottey. Besides being quite attractive and "hilarious," Krista runs a Southern California boutique with her cousin (". . . tongues are mercilessly wagging that it was the People's Champ who funded Krista's new boutique," reported the *Star*, which regularly writes about Krista and Pacquiao and then righteously says she should be left alone.

On one of the more traditional news sites, ABS-CBNnews.com reported that Jinkee said, "For my family, for my children, I will survive. I need to surpass every challenge. I need to be strong. God is just testing us. I know the Lord wants us to be together." She also said that she hoped the public would put rumors of Manny Pacquiao's extra-marital affairs to rest. "That's done. It has a period at the end. There are no question marks in the minds of the people." Asked how much he loves his wife, Pacquiao answered, "Of course, I really love her. She's my wife. We have many children." The ongoing soap opera fascinates the public.

Pacquiao is a professional athlete. "He works hard, and he plays hard," Filipino men always tell me. Among some Filipinos, infidelity is almost an accepted fact of life. Families tend to stick together in the staunchly Catholic country where divorce is for all intents and purposes illegal. Infidelity has its so-called risks—it's practically easier to buy a gun than a condom. Someone close to Pacquiao tells me, "The trials they go through as a couple, with the fame and fortune and the girls swooning over him—the tough times they have had, will keep them together. There comes a time when men will look in the other direction when the wife becomes heavier on the sides and she grows old, and here comes popularity and fame and you have girls who you never dreamed of meeting in your life, falling by your wayside. Here is a guy who grew up adoring movie personalities. Now these girls are swooning over him. Maybe it's part of his growth as a person."

Pacquiao can come across as a loving husband. On HBO's *24/7* he is shown wearing headphones. He has a device on his wife's pregnant belly so he can listen to his unborn child's heartbeat. "Hello, talk to me," he says to the baby. Pacquiao giggles. Jinkee laughs. And they kiss. This was before his youngest daughter was born. He has his kids' names—Jimuel, Michael, Princess, and Queen Elizabeth—tattooed on his left arm. He is a caring father, but Manny Pacquiao's life is complicated and obsessed over by his public.

People will talk about Manny freely and discuss his foibles, and even when extramarital affairs are not brought up, everyone else—men and women—seem to want to talk about starlets, the girl he was supposedly caught French kissing as he came out of a Manila club ("She was a fan"), the whispers about Brazilian models, and Jinkee's crying fits. Some Filipinos don't seem to care about the morality of this sort of stuff—*boys will be boys*—but Pacquiao is the greatest thing to ever happen to the country, so they are worried that it might just bring him down. Given the constant attention he receives, the relentless newspaper speculation is seriously embarrassing for his wife—people feel like she deserves more respect. (After Pacquiao's friends start blabbering about his female friends, I am given a standard line, "Don't quote me on the women!")

While I am in the Philippines, I happen to have a drink at the Mandarin Oriental in Manila's Makati district. Unprompted, a regular patron says Pacquiao is a frequent visitor to Martini's, the hotel bar. There is a definite man-code in play. "He is a good guy," a worker tells me, sort of straining himself to let me—hint, hint—get the drift. "He. Is. A. Man." Being a man in the Filipino culture can mean serious side action. "We are a culture that when a business deal is signed, a naked woman will be given as a gift," an American-educated, Manila-based Filipino told me.

Anyone who deems to write about Pacquiao's supposed mistress(es) tends to be denied any access to him. Filipino gossip columnists dissect Manny and Jinkee's every move and desperately ply the sports journalists for inside information. There is a tremendous amount of disdain from the sportswriters, of course. Revealing Pacquiao's personal life is a good way to get kicked out of the Pacquiao camp. The sports journalists are refreshingly old-fashioned when it comes to privacy.

Recah Trinidad, dryly humorous, collected his reporting about Pacquiao in a slim and incisive 2006 book, *Pacific Storm: Dispatches on Pacquiao of the Philippines*. The carefully crafted columns were laudatory about the National Fist. But Trinidad, a serious journalist, decided to print the entire affidavit and counteraffidavit of a paternity suit. It gave people a whiff of impropriety as it described how one Joanna Rose Bacosa and Pacquiao carried on an affair. By trade a "billiard spotter and waitress," according to the lawsuit, Bacosa worked in Manila's Pan Pacific Hotel. Pacquiao, a devoted billiards player, was there almost every night, according to Bacosa. One thing led to another and the two started having sex. He was a caring boyfriend, and even surprised her on her birthday. She got pregnant. Pacquiao, according to her, was pleased and enjoyed kissing her tummy. The baby boy, named after him, was born in 2004. He rented her an apartment, gave her money, and then seemed to lose interest. He started frequenting another pool hall, "Rock & Roll Billiards." Going broke, Bacosa claimed that Pacquiao refused to support her and became upset when she started telling people about the affair. She alleged in the lawsuit that he called her and said, "What do you want? Financial support? What if I have the child kidnapped so there is no evidence?" She answered, "Don't talk like that. I only want a good life for my child." Then came his warning: "Talk to your lawyer. Tell him to shut up, or I'll sew up his mouth."

Pacquiao filed a counteraffidavit saying, "That whether Joanna Rose Bacosa and I indulged or not in sex, is immaterial or inappropriate to solve the questions raised in this complaint. . . . All the accusations of Bacosa are not true. I can't imagine how she did this in spite of the assistance I have given her and her baby."

This being the Philippines, the alleged affair reached the country's highest office. The president's husband ("the First Gentleman") went on national television. He was grim-faced. "Why are they doing this to Manny, instead of honoring and protecting him. Why are they destroying him?"

Jinkee, gracious and dutifully forgiving, said, "I think he already learned from his mistakes. All I can say is I am Manny's number one; nobody can contest that. He's very loving, and lovable."

IN 2006, the *New York Times* ran an obituary of Betty Friedan, author of *The Feminine Mystique*, which "ignited the contemporary women's movement in 1963 and as a result permanently transformed the social fabric of the United States and countries around the world." *Around the world. . . .* The obituary writer has obviously never been to the Philippines or to Glendale, California, on Valentine's Day. On one spring afternoon several hundred Filipinas dragged their husbands and kids to a hotel ballroom for the event, "Manny Pacquiao Shows His Love."

Of course, Manny is late. To be exact, he is two hours, twenty-seven minutes, and thirteen seconds late. Each of the five hundred people paid twenty dollars to get a glimpse of their idol, and they wait placidly, some slowly getting drunk and enduring a string of Pinoy rock bands and torch singers, which alternate between family music (one guy is belting out the Filipino version of "Do Re Mi"), the religious, and the sexually suggestive (one young Filipina with bleached hair, black tights, and red shorts sings a suggestive and throaty version of "Chain of Fools"—"Manny Pacquiao, I thought you were my man . . . ") That Manny is routinely late, even by three or four hours, doesn't seem to raise an eyebrow. Waiting, it seems, is a regular part of life. His fans are used to it, and the little kids wile away the time by sleeping or sitting patiently, their parents ask, "Aren't you excited to see Manny?" in Tagalog or Visyan or English.

There is a lot of chitchat about Manny being a "noble man," too. In what seems like a clever way of getting rid of old Pacquiao merchandise, memorabilia—such as T-shirts, posters, boxing gloves, and other items—from previous fights are sold at small stands in the back of the room, undoubtedly the handiwork of someone in the entourage. The event had been pitched as a way for fans to see him and maybe even get a picture or autograph on Valentine's Day, a day that seems to hold fantastical significance to Filipinas. "Manny will only be signing memorabilia bought in the ballroom!" someone roars. Some of his handlers aren't sure exactly where the greatest boxer in the world had been since they put him on a private plane out of Las Vegas last night, but the front door finally opens into the ballroom, and the crazed crowd of Manny fans scrambles to their feet. At least a quarter of the crowd were older ladies, and they look the most visibly excited, some shaking. Filipino mothers are used to seeing their children leave for far-off destinations, and so they tend to look at Manny as their own lost son. When he strolls through the door, the elfin ladies desperately and furiously climb on chairs, holding their cameras aloft. There are screams all around, "Sit down! Sit down! We paid our twenty dollars, too!"

Manny climbs on the dais and looks a little confused. So many people stand and take photographs that there is a murmur of dissent through the crowd. They *have* to see their idol! And who can blame them as they've been waiting for hours in anticipation of Pacquiao's presence. News crews from the Philippines and a couple of the local Los Angeles stations are here because *any* Pacquiao coverage in the Los Angeles Basin is gold in the ratings.

Manny says something in Filipino that no one can seem to understand (mic problems), and then in English he says, "Thank you, for all your support." It is an awfully short, poorly prepared speech. He is wearing a short-sleeved checkered shirt and a Nike hoodie. Some obnoxious person close to him grabs the microphone and blares, "We are auctioning off Manny's jacket! Bidding starts at $210; it is for a good cause." No one seems to know the cause, but the hoodie bidding gets up to $450. Pacquiao looks uneasy and grabs a pen and jokes, "Why don't we auction off this, too?"

The autograph signing eventually takes place, and the women have their chance to get close to the country's male role icon, shyly standing next to him and sweetly nodding, as many Filipinos tend to do. Women accept their "traditional" (and, by Western standards, passive) role.

Outside of the Glendale Embassy Suites, I see Michael Koncz, sitting across from the valet, smoking a cigarette. Koncz! He looks like he might not have had a chance to change his clothes in the last forty-eight hours. He is just back from Vegas where Pacquiao was promoting a boxing event, PINOY POWER! "Our boxer won," he says, in a scratchy, tired voice. That's about all I get. He doesn't look like he wants to talk with me, as writers are not really Koncz's favorite people. Koncz has his detractors (his inability to return phone calls among other traits hardly endears him to reporters), but he is known for his fierce loyalty to Manny Pacquiao. "Manny trusts him; he doesn't steal from him," says Ronnie Nathanielsz.

MANNY PACQUIAO sits in a pew seven rows from the back in Hollywood's Christ the King Church. His knees rest on the kneeler, and his hands are clasped together. It is Sunday morning, 8:47 a.m., the Third Sunday of Lent, and his wife, Jinkee, sits next to him, and so does his aunt. The couple is in a state of prayer. Of course there is nothing really private or anonymous about it. Pacquiao's videographer is shooting the scene, and people are craning their necks to see the world champion. Buboy is in the very back, standing during the entire service.

The Church is packed, seven hundred strong. Three-quarters of the people are Filipinos, and there are some Hispanics, whites, and African Americans thrown in for good measure. People kneel down to a portrait of Saint Kowalska, the Polish nun, who in the 1930s, said she spoke to Jesus and Mary. Worshippers cross themselves underneath a portrait of Christ.

Many members of the entourage are present.

Manny's voice coach, who leads the choir, sings: "Gather your people, O Lord . . . One bread, one body, one spirit of love . . . "

Pacquiao and his family go to communion. Pacquiao returns and clasps his hand together again. The rest of the congregation listens to the words of the priest, who talks about how he will be leaving the church to take another assignment, someone from the church's school brandishes a trophy and talks about the school's accomplishments in a recent academic competition, and a group of children sing. Pacquiao's head stays down. Is he praying? Soon, he will be getting on his private jet with 132 members of his entourage, only a handful of whom he actually knows, and head for his next fight. He continues to bow his head until the priest asks him and Jinkee to come to the altar for a blessing. He asks the congregation to pray for Pacquiao.

"Hail Mary, full of grace . . . "

8

THE MEXICUTIONER

MEXICO'S INSECURITIES and poverty—not unlike that of the Philippines—tends to create boxing warriors who are not only willing to die in the ring, but who have the technical skills to back up their courage. There are a lot of pros and cons to bringing American kids up through an amateur system, but the Philippines, Mexico, and Puerto Rico, all boxing powerhouses, are not really known for great amateur world champions or Olympic medalists. Young fighters go into gyms, littered across each respective country, where veteran trainers are on the hunt for the next Julio Cesar Chavez, Felix Trinidad, or Manny Pacquiao. Mexico takes its boxing very seriously: Its name fighters are actual stars and usually come from its poorest areas, a typical breeding ground for most boxers in the world. Given its historically dire economic state, Mexico has created some of the best and most numerous champions. Pacquiao always wanted to fight the men who he had come to admire. At the turn of the last century, Mexicans—and about everyone else—still didn't really know anything about Manny Pacquiao.

In the last two decades, the flyweight to welterweight divisions (112 pounds to 147 pounds) have been loaded with talent. These divisions have included Mexican battlers and cultural icons such as Marco Antonio Barrera, Juan Manuel Marquez, David Díaz, Erik Morales, and—the ultimate test—Oscar De La Hoya, an American of Mexican origins, who no one in his right mind would ever dream of matching with Pacquiao, who was five inches shorter and twenty pounds lighter. Not only did these fighters have ring bravery to match Pacquiao's nearly suicidal aggression, but they were technicians par excellence.

Was Pacquiao ready for the Mexican demigods? And would he be able to draw enough fans to make the fights worthwhile for his promoters?

As a Filipino who spoke a strained brand of English, Manny Pacquiao was hardly a major North American media attraction. Promoters often sell fights on racial animosity, but there is not a great deal of enmity between Filipinos and Mexicans. There was, however, popular momentum building for Pacquiao. As the calendar turned to 2001, HBO was following him more closely. Five months after his victory over Lehlohonolo Ledwaba of South Africa, he took on Agapito Sanchez, the WBO titleholder, at the Bill Graham Civic Auditorium in San Francisco. (Floyd Mayweather was fighting the main event, a WBC super featherweight bout against Jesús Chávez.) The Bay Area has a sizeable Filipino population, so the place was packed. It was a unification bout that pitted two good, young fighters, but it turned out to be an ugly one with Pacquiao sustaining a head butt in rounds two and six (smaller fighters often use their heads to lead into a punch, thus causing

Photograph by
Nana Buxani

ABOVE: Pacquiao grew up in abject poverty in the Philippines. He lived in a cardboard shack, missed many meals, and was forced to quit school in sixth grade so he could earn money for his family.

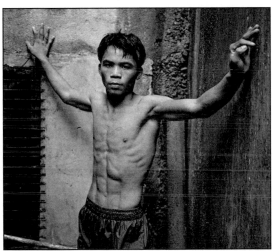

LEFT: Pacquiao was a teenager at Manila's L&M Gym. A young Pacquiao left the southern Philippines for the nation's capital. He honed his skills in the boxing gym and worked a variety of labor jobs to survive. He turned pro at sixteen as a light flyweight—at just 106 pounds.

Photographs left and below:
© Gerhard Joren/OnAsia.com

RIGHT: Boxers at the L&M gym in Manila in 1996. Manny Pacquiao is second from the right behind the heavy bag. Some of the boxers, including Manny, would sleep in the small closetlike rooms in the back of the gym, which was known for its oppressive heat.

Photograph by Nana Buxani

Photograph by Gary Andrew Poole

TOP: Millions of people participate in the annual procession of the Black Nazarene. Manny Pacquiao, deeply religious, is a devotee of the idol. Filipinos liken their poverty and struggles to the tribulations experienced by Jesus. BOTTOM: Cockfighting is a popular sport in the Philippines, and Pacquiao owns many fighting roosters. Pictured is a cockfight near his birthplace in Mindanao.

Photograph by Chris Farina

Photograph by Gary Andrew Poole

TOP: After Pacquiao started working with hall of fame trainer Freddie Roach, the PacMan developed into one of the greatest boxers of all time. Roach has Parkinson's disease. BOTTOM: Pacquiao is known for his incredibly fast hands. Boxing historian Bert Sugar says, "They are the fastest hands I have ever seen."

Photograph by Chris Farina

Photograph by Jay Directo/AFP/Getty Images

TOP: Outside of the ring, Pacquiao is known for all-night sessions of singing and carousing, and playing billiards, poker, chess, and the piano. BOTTOM: Manny Pacquiao, his wife Jinkee, and three of his children arrive at Manila International Airport. Pacquiao is a cultural icon in the Philippines, and he is mobbed everywhere he goes in the world.

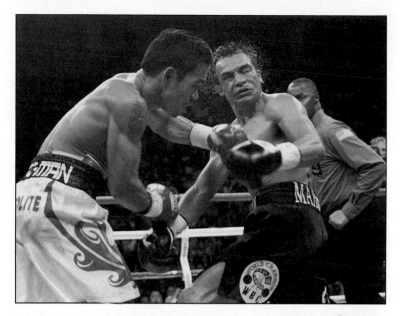

Photographs by Chris Farina

TOP: In 2004, Pacquiao fought Mexican champion Juan Manuel Marquez with the world featherweight title on the line. The PacMan knocked down Marquez three times, but the Mexican came back to earn a controversial draw. Four years later, in a rematch that also went the distance, Pacquiao won in a controversial split decision—giving Pacquiao the super featherweight title. BOTTOM: Pacquiao met Mexican Erik Morales in March 2005 and lost in a unanimous twelve-round decision. The defeat prompted Pacquiao to become a more complete boxer. He would fight Morales three times, beating him twice in 2006—the first by TKO, the second by knockout.

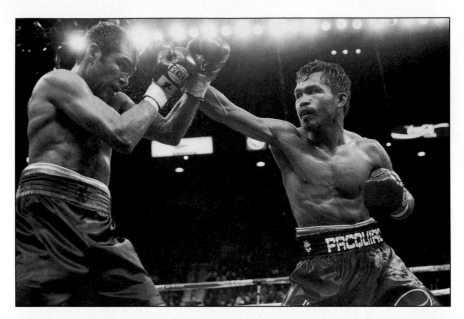

Photographs by Chris Farina

TOP: Coming into the 2008 duel with Mexican American icon Oscar De La Hoya, Pacquiao was a decisive underdog. Pacquiao dominated the Golden Boy, forcing his corner to throw in the towel after the eighth round. It was a stunning win. De La Hoya retired after the bout. BOTTOM: Pacquiao's devastating knockout of the English champion Ricky Hatton on May 2, 2009, has been described as the greatest punch since Rocky Marciano KO'd Jersey Joe Walcott in 1952.

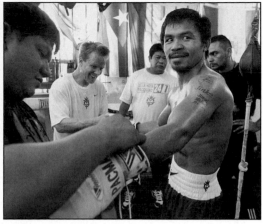

Alex Ariza (ABOVE LEFT), Pacquiao's conditioning coach, has helped the PacMan retain his speed and power as the Filipino has risen to fight bigger opponents. (ABOVE RIGHT) Buboy Fernandez, Pacquiao's childhood friend, laces up the champ's gloves at the Wild Card Boxing Club.

Photographs by Chris Farina

ABOVE: Pacquiao's win over Puerto Rican superstar Miguel Cotto in 2009 gave the PacMan an unprecedented seven world titles in seven divisions.

Photograph by Chris Farina

ABOVE: Trainer Freddie Roach, Pacquiao's promoter Bob Arum, and the champion. BELOW: When Pacquiao campaigned for Congress in 2010, thousands of adoring fans would come listen to their idol's speeches, in which he talked about his own impoverished youth. He won the election.

Photograph by Jay Directo/AFP/Getty Images

a clash of heads). Sanchez also lost points for a series of low blows. To the grave disappointment of his management team, the bout was ultimately declared a draw. Still, Pacquiao was a comer. Now his managers had their eyes on an extraordinary group of Mexican fighters who they felt Pacquiao could vanquish on the way to future lucrative paydays.

BARRERA I

PACQUIAO WAS a four-to-one underdog (in boxing those are especially long odds) going into his November 2003 fight against Marco Antonio Barrera. Pacquiao's draw against unheralded Sanchez certainly didn't help his cause. Bettors also couldn't get past the fact that Pacquiao was barely a junior featherweight, and he would be jumping up four pounds to featherweight—a natural poundage for the Mexican. Besides the size advantage, Barrera, an efficient boxer, was in a completely different class of any fighter than Pacquiao had previously faced. Many boxing historians put the Mexican in the top fifty fighters of all time. After recording an amateur record of 56–4, including winning the Mexican national championship five times, he turned professional at the age of fifteen and quickly dismantled his opponents with a full-on attacking style. He became a seven-time world champion in three different weight classes.

Before the fight, Pacquiao trained in a small gym in San Antonio. (Top Rank's boxing publicist Bill Caplan remembers meeting him for the first time in the gym, "That smile hasn't changed. Pretty much the same guy, except he is more worldly now.") Pacquiao rode in a taxi to San Antonio's Alamodome for the fight. He entered the ring wearing a Tim Duncan San Antonio Spurs jersey to elicit some hometown sympathy. Nonetheless, the pro-Barrera crowd booed him lustily. Oscar De La Hoya and his business partner Richard Schaefer sat ringside. Barrera was a Golden Boy client. Schaefer expected an easy win. "It was a shock," Schaefer says. "We couldn't believe our eyes. I really wasn't worried about the fight going in. Everyone was telling me it was going to be a walk in the park for Barrera. It was anything but."

Both men had seen Pacquiao fight before. It was in June 2001 when Pacquiao appeared on the undercard the night De La Hoya earned a twelve-round unanimous decision over Javier Castillejo at the MGM Grand. They had been impressed with how Pacquiao had beaten Lehlohonolo Ledwaba for the IBF super bantamweight title that night. But Ledwaba was no Barrera. Just prior to the bout, it was revealed that Barrera had undergone surgery to repair a cluster of malformed blood vessels in his head, but no one seemed overly concerned, especially when less than a minute into the fight, Pacquiao fell to the canvas. Referee Laurence Cole gave Pacquiao a standing eight count. The ten thousand spectators dutifully cheered. But Pacquiao gamely jumped off the canvas and started fighting. Roach's game plan coming into the bout was stay close, give no quarter, and hammer him with body shots. Pacquiao started executing the plan. In the third round, Pacquiao landed a left that took Barrera down. He tried to regain his senses. The crowd quieted. Down at ringside, Schaefer's eyes followed Barrera to his corner. By the end of the eleventh round, a humbled Barrera had been bludgeoned into submission. Pacquiao had landed 150 more power punches than the Mexican. The referee stopped the fight, and Pacquiao raised his arms, crying and smiling as his corner men draped the Philippine flag around his shoulders. "At least they're finally beginning to pronounce his name right," said Rod Nazario in a reference to HBO's announcers consistently mispronouncing Pacquiao's name. *Ring* magazine, the so-called bible of boxing, named Pacquiao the featherweight champion of the world.

The night after the fight, Pacquiao underwent a major spiritual transformation. Commentators note how Pacquiao enters the ring with a blissful joy and pre-fight he appears to have a Zen-like calm spread across his face. He says God possesses him. With his dramatic victory over Barrera, it forced him to think about who he was, and who he wanted to be. Many fighters won't sleep after a fight. They say the adrenaline rush will kill you. When Pacquiao eventually drifted off, he told friends how God's messenger had talked to him in a dream, told him to mend his ways. Pacquiao awoke in the night and he was crying. He decided to re-devote himself to his faith.

When he returned to Manila, hundreds of thousands turned out to cheer his motorcade. "*Hindi ko akalain na gan-ito karami ang sasalubong sa akin dito sa Maynila, talagang nakakataba ng puso* (I did not expect so many people to come out and welcome me, I'm really touched)," he said. He filmed some commercials and a movie, collected awards, attended parties in his honor, and campaigned for President Gloria Macapagal Arroyo in the nation's election. His purse for the Barrera fight was $700,000, but Pacquiao knew subsequent fights could earn him well more than $1 million per fight. Pacquiao went on a spending spree. He bought $15,000 watches, two houses (one in General Santos City, the other in Davao), and cars (a Honda SUV, a Ford Expedition, and a Toyota Tamaraw). The entourage started getting bigger and bigger. (Nazario told *Time* that he remembers calling Pacquiao the morning after a party in his honor, not long after the fighter returned from the United States. "He said, 'I thought I had thirty relatives,'" Nazario recalls, "'but there were actually one hundred . . . 150 . . . 200 . . . and they all say they are my relatives!'") Even then, people were worried about his over-generosity, which seemed to many to border on naïveté. "I don't mind having these relatives," he said. "I'll give them a little, since they all prayed for my victory."

Pacquiao, hinting at his political ambitions, used his new platform to appeal for Filipino unity and an end to corruption. The Philippines is a place in which there are thousands of islands and thousands of dialects, not to mention fiefdoms throughout the archipelago. Pacquiao's statements about unity were not really taken seriously. Though a national icon already, he was a mere boxer. Many Filipinos wanted him to remain their "idol," and stay away from political talk.

JUAN MANUEL MARQUEZ I

PACQUIAO WAS SPENDING more and more time in General Santos, which was more hectic than his relatively anonymous Los Angeles existence. His pride and joy was a $54,000 mansion—complete with a boxing glove–shaped swimming pool. He also started having a house built nearby for his mother. But his fame brought problems. His mother was robbed. To keep them away from the hands of kidnappers,

Pacquiao's two sons, Emmanuel Junior and Michael, lived behind the tall walls surrounding his palace and security guards were employed to protect his immediate family. Pacquiao had won a significant fight, but his inner circle started worrying about his focus. His next bout would be in May 2004 against another accomplished Mexican, Juan Manuel Marquez, an IBF and WBC featherweight champ, who many considered one of the best pound-for-pound fighters in the world. While Pacquiao was relaxing at home and hanging out in pool halls, Marquez had already started training, telling reporters, "Only in death will I relinquish my belts."

Pacquiao had suffered so much in life that enablers in his circle felt he deserved a break. To the people who had been with him since the beginning—and who felt he could accomplish even bigger things—it felt like 1995 all over again. That was the year that Pacquiao became so over-confident that he lost to Rustico Torrecampo, the gym hand who had knocked him cold with a third-round punch. And Juan Manuel Marquez was no gym hand.

EVEN BY THE STANDARDS of boxing, Juan Manuel Marquez has some screwy habits. In training, he eats raw quail eggs and drinks his own piss because "a lot of proteins and vitamins are part of your vitamin intake, and *why not drink them again?*" Marquez, predictably, had a tough upbringing. He was one of eight children born to a former pro fighter in the Mexico City barrio of Iztapalapa. As a youngster, his father strapped pillows to his body and taught him how to spar. Marquez had built his reputation up over the years, and he was upset at the attention Pacquiao received from fans and the media. And in Las Vegas the Filipino was a nine-to-five betting favorite.

Pacquiao's fight against the Mexican dual world champion was held on a spring Saturday evening in Las Vegas. There were 7,129 at the MGM Grand. It began in a flourish as Pacquiao floored Marquez three times in the first round, landing powerful straight lefts. The *Los Angeles Times* wrote about the successful punches, "It was so basic it was beautiful. A simple right jab followed by a thunderous and heavy-handed left cross." After round one, the World Boxing Association and the IBF champion was hit by the same punch for the third time. He went flat on his back. He barely beat the count. It looked like it would be an early night. Marquez knew the punches were coming, but Pacquiao was just too quick.

But one of the blows also injured Pacquiao's hand, which throbbed and started to swell. (*Putang ina Aray!* SOB Ouch!) His footwork didn't seem right, either. He had a badly blistered right toe, which he was favoring and cramps in his left leg. Marquez became emboldened and fought back.

Pacquiao was unable to put down Marquez, a notoriously slow starter, in round two. The Mexican was glassy-eyed but savvy enough to adjust to Pacquiao as he started picking off the PacMan's weakening left by raising his right glove. Pacquiao was genuinely shocked that he hadn't already won the fight.

In round three, Marquez came back in earnest. "In the first round, I got careless and got hit with a right hand," said the Mexican, who bled from both nostrils from the first round on and was obviously still feeling the effects of the lefts that dropped him. "The plan was to box carefully, and I didn't do it. I was disoriented after the first round, but once I got my head clear, I thought I won all the other rounds, except possibly one round."

In round five, Marquez delivered a stiff left, which caused a gash over Pacquiao's right eye. The men exchanged a flurry of punches. There was nationalistic fervor in the arena: Mexican fans serenaded Marquez, *"Si, se puede"* ("Yes, we can"), as he landed scoring blows, mostly counter rights to the face. The Filipinos were furiously waving the red, blue, white, and yellow national flag.

After twelve action-packed rounds—they combined to throw 1,186 punches with Marquez landing 29 percent (158 of 547) and Pacquiao 23 percent (148 of 639). Michael Buffer read the scores. Judge Burt Clements scored the bout 113–113, Guy Jutras had it 115–110 in favor of Marquez, and John Stewart scored it 115–110 for Pacquiao.

Draw.

"Obviously, I thought I won, and I didn't think it was close," said a disappointed Pacquiao. "I thought I took [Marquez's] fight away from him."

Then Pacquiao began to sniffle and then wept openly. He said he had failed his countrymen.

With the draw, Marquez retained his belts and his record moved to 42–2–1.

Marquez showed up at the postfight press conference with a misshapen face, claiming the judges had robbed him. He intermittently put an ice bag on his mouth. Pacquiao came with a wound over the right eye and bruises on his forehead and cheeks.

Freddie Roach said Pacquiao failed to give 100 percent due to his injuries and rabid desire to score a knockout.

"But he definitely did enough to win the fight," said Roach.

There was talk of a rematch. Marquez wasn't so sure he wanted one yet. Pacquiao was pleading to go again.

IN TRAVEL OFFICES around the world, agents were noticing an uptick in Filipino travel to specific destinations, particularly Las Vegas. They would come to the Filipino mecca of California and endure family and then travel to watch Pacquiao, usually traveling halfway around the world to watch the bout on closed-circuit television because high rollers get the majority of the tickets at major Vegas fights. It became a family ritual. For the Marquez bout, Filipino families seemed to be everywhere in the casinos. There was swelling passion for Pacquiao. Promoters and network executives believed Pacquiao had brought a new audience to the sport, not just Filipinos, but white Americans. Pacquiao was almost perceived as a mixed-martial-arts guy in a boxing ring. His kinetic, all-out style made him marketable to the video game generation. Mixed martial arts had been luring white America away from boxing. When it began in 1993, the first UFC was meant to be a gimmicky showcase for Brazilian-style Jiu-Jitsu, and rowdy audiences screamed for matchups of pugilists against wrestlers against kickboxers. The cage surrounding the ring was intended to keep the audiences from jumping in as much as to keep the fighters from falling out. Senator John McCain and others attacked the sport. Then, in 2001, Frank Fertitta III and his brother

Lorenzo, entrepreneurs in the Las Vegas casino business, bought the tarnished name Ultimate Fighting Championship and rehabilitated the sport. Technically called mixed martial arts, ultimate fighting was given a set of rules (no more head butting) and a synthesis of fighting styles. A doctor was stationed ringside to discourage death, and a referee joined the fighters within to break up dangerous holds, penalize illegal blows, and stop the action if necessary. Dana White, an ex-boxing manager, joined as president. He was a master marketer and helped create a popular reality show—*The Ultimate Fighter*—on Spike TV, which is popular with young American men. It featured MMA fighters who were training, as well as infighting, engaging in drunken frolics, not to mention bashing in doors, and one competitor urinating on another's bed. "*The Ultimate Fighter* was our Trojan horse," says White. ("It's the right show for the right network," Kevin Kay, executive vice president for programming and production at Spike TV told me back in 2005. Says Kay, who helped develop *SpongeBob SquarePants* for Nickelodeon: "I was skeptical at first, but I just love it.")

At the time, boxing was considered by the media and by much of the public as a completely lost cause. Everyone was looking to Oscar De La Hoya, who was on the downward slope of his career, or Floyd Mayweather Jr., a technically brilliant boxer who possessed an utterly boring, defensive style, to revive the sweet science. Pacquiao was someone who promoters could sell. He had a backstory and was a boxer who was always on the offensive. He made moves like an NBA player taking it to the hoop. His lunging lefts carried enormous high risk and high drama. His attitude in and outside of the ring was also starting to intrigue people who had given up on boxing sometime around the year that Mike Tyson bit off Evander Holyfield's earlobe.

Pacquiao, who some call "boxing's Bruce Lee," just seemed different and fresh. While many boxers and promoters talk about the importance of pushing undefeated fighters onto the viewing public, the public seemed unconcerned about "0's" (many of the most popular MMA fighters have lost fights). Pacquiao wanted to please the fans and played by a completely different set of rules. His reputation for humility, a trait praised in MMA, also set him apart. UFC president Dana White, who likes to criticize boxing, readily admits that he is a Pacquiao fan.

ERIK MORALES I

WHEN PACQUIAO RETURNED to Los Angeles in the spring of 2004 to train, Roach began the camp by teaching Pacquiao some techniques on how to better cut off the ring with his footwork. Pacquiao's feet are so deceptively quick that it is difficult for opponents to keep up with the pace and shiftiness. But Pacquiao could also be predictable, not really taking advantage of his lateral quickness. Roach was also trying to get Pacquiao to become more balanced. Like a basketball player who constantly shoots fadeaway jumpers, Pacquiao tended to move forward after throwing a punch and get slightly off balance as he threw his second punch in a combination, which would shortchange the power of his strike. Roach worked with Pacquiao to distribute his weight more evenly so he could throw more power punches. After a week under Roach's tutelage, Pacquiao started sparring. In the first session, he beat up Armenian Karen Harutyunyan so badly that the unbeaten bantamweight with a career mark of ten wins and three draws went home with a brace and an ice pack on his chest. The Armenian suffered a bruised left rib and had to get two X-rays to make sure there were no broken bones in his body.

Pacquiao continued to improve, but behind the scenes there was turmoil in Pacquiao's camp. Roach was becoming upset with Pacquiao's management team. He threatened to quit because he was unhappy with promoter Murad Muhammad over money matters. Muhammad, at age sixteen, started following Muhammad Ali around and eventually became his personal security detail. (Muhammad favors custom-made shirts, pinstriped suits, and hats with a showy feather at the side.) Roach and Muhammad wrangled over Manny and larger cuts of Pacquiao's purses. Within the boxing community, there were numerous people who didn't like that Roach was taking Muhammad to task. It is an unwritten law that trainers train, not manage. But Roach felt that Pacquiao was vulnerable. Roach would tell him to fire someone detrimental to his career, but Pacquiao just couldn't do it. The matter with his management team was different because it was also jeopardizing his relationship with Roach, who he was starting to see as something more than just a trainer. "Freddie is like a father, a brother, and a friend," says Pacquiao. "He is good. I learned so much from him. We like each other, and we are lucky for each other."

Roach deals with many fascinating personalities, juggling the demands of promoters, fighters, the media, television executives, boxing commission reps, Hollywood celebrities, friends, and family. Considering that he lives and dies to be in his gym training fighters, he navigates the competing interests pretty well. Most of all, he is loyal to his fighters. He understands them, and he cares about them. He laughs about fighters being headcases and talks about how he used to get out of bed every morning by superstitiously putting his left foot on the floor first. Fighters, "practitioners in the hurt business," need things just so. As time goes by in a boxer's life, they seem to get more and more insanely superstitious.

In the prefight press conference, the Erik Morales camp mocked Pacquiao and dared his entourage, which now had more and more Los Angeles-based hangers-on, to take a $100,000 bet. They didn't take it. Then Murad Muhammad gave a long-winded speech, and the crowd jeered him.

The extracurricular stuff turns boxing into a ludicrous sideshow much of the time. Roach is used to the histrionics of his sport, but he felt there was too much freak show as March 19, 2005, approached. Morales could backup his team's trash talk: He ranks No. 49 on ESPN's "50 Greatest Boxers of All Time" list, a slot ahead of Mike Tyson. The Tijuana-born pro won five world championship titles. The handsome Morales didn't really enter a ring as much as he swaggered into the square-circle. Roach had started working on Pacquiao's right hand, which they had nicknamed Manila Ice. But it was still in the developing stages. Roach knew going into the fight that Pacquiao was hardly a complete fighter, and he was fighting at 130 pounds for the first time. After the weigh-in and numerous slurps of Filipino soup, Pacquiao would come into the bout weighing 136 pounds; Morales would use the day after weigh-in to hydrate and eat and get up to 143 pounds by fight time, which is a significant advantage in a sport in which every pound can make a boxer that much more powerful. The boxing commission had fouled up Pacquiao's drug test so the Filipino had to give blood before the fight. This was bad. Pacquiao lives in daily chaos, but he swears by a regular routine. Pacquiao believed that releasing blood weakened his spirit. Usually good-natured before a fight, he complained that he didn't feel good. Capping off the bad news, Murad Muhammad had made an agreement that Pacquiao would fight with Winning gloves, a thick and foamy Japanese brand, different from Pacquiao's favored pair, which are Cleto Reyes gloves, known as punchers' gloves filled with horsehair so the wearer can make a tighter fist. ("I would never allow my fighter to be disadvantaged," said Muhammad. Everyone seemed to think Muhammad had been snookered.) Fighters want everything just so, but the lead up to the fight was too unpredictable for the PacMan's liking.

After a flourish of punches from Morales in round two, Pacquiao held out his hands as if to say, "Bring it on." It didn't seem like El Terrible could hurt the Filipino, who wore red shorts with yellow flames. Morales, wearing white trunks, backed away, using the strategy of a counterpuncher. No one had ever seen Erik Morales back away quite so much. It was a clever strategy because Morales didn't want to compete against Pacquiao's handspeed. Let Pacquiao punch himself out, grow fatigued, and become frustrated in the later rounds so the thinking went.

At the end of round two, Pacquiao came to the corner. He was grinning joyfully. He was enjoying himself. The brawl was very close, and there was a constant buzz of noise from the people in the MGM Grand.

Roach sensed overconfidence: "After you throw your combinations, you can't stand in front of this guy, okay? Ya gotta use your speed." Pacquiao still had the tendency to stand straight up and not duck away after unleashing a flurry of punches. "Deep breath. Vaseline." Roach applied it himself. He likes to do all the dirty work because he says a fighter trusts him more if he does most of the corner scutwork himself.

Morales's counterpunching was close to brilliant. He let Pacquiao come in, and then he turned around with precise straight rights. Manila Ice wasn't working. The Mexican won round three.

Roach: "Manny, don't take this guy lightly. When you get him on the ropes, take advantage of him."

"Okay."

Pacquiao breathed heavily.

By round four, Pacquiao was getting trapped on the ropes as Morales hit him with a slew of punches, from his belly button to his head. In between rounds, Pacquiao spit blood into the white bucket. Morales seemed to be taking Pacquiao's punches without much concern. Pacquiao relied on his quick hands, but that wasn't enough against a guy like Morales, who was able to take one or two glancing blows and then return fire with harder shots to Pacquiao's frame.

In round five, a cut above Pacquiao's right eye opened up. While the referee said it was caused by a punch, the replays showed that it was an accidental headbutt. It was gruesome.

Half of his face was covered with blood. He could barely see, and it seemed to impact his footwork most of all. Pacquiao couldn't see the oncoming punches and stumbled several times. Into round five of the super-featherweight showdown, ringside physician William Capanna looked into the eyes of Pacquiao and asked him if he wanted to continue. One eye stared back. The cut was deep, and blood continued to cavalcade down his face. He told Capanna he could go on, no problem. Buboy Fernandez, freaking out, urged Pacquiao to knock out the Mexican. He was behind on all three judges' scorecards. Morales, traditionally a slow starter, had matched Pacquiao's furious pace.

In the corner, the cutman went to work. Roach calmly told everyone to settle down and plotted strategy. "Deep breath, son," he said. "Back him up with combinations."

Pacquiao went for the knockout. He came forward relentlessly, desperately. Morales was taller and had a longer reach. Pacquiao was in trouble.

"You have got to back this guy up," Roach said.

The men exchanged shots for the next several rounds. Pacquiao would come at the Mexican with four-part combinations; Morales would return fire with jabs and right-hand leads. Some of the body shots crumpled Pacquiao, who found it within himself to continue fighting at a furious pace. He couldn't see out of one eye, but he was able to wobble Morales in the ninth. Roach told him to keep backing up Morales. "All right," Pacquiao said, politely.

It was close, most experts giving the edge to Morales, and so in the twelfth round Pacquiao needed a knockout. For some reason, Morales switched to a southpaw style and Pacquiao pounced, boring in and hitting him directly and hard.

Everyone stood up.

It was a hell of a brawl.

The sellout crowd of 14,623 stood and cheered through most of it. Morales could have taken the last round off, but he went toe-to-toe, showing that he could withstand Pacquiao's barrage of punches, mostly lefts. They both tasted a lot of leather. Pacquiao's urine would still have blood in it a week after the fight.

AFTER THE SCORE was announced. Pacquiao leaned into Buboy and cried.

Morales: "He was a tough guy; I hit him with everything."

Morales had won a close, but unanimous decision. All three judges—Paul Smith, Dave Moretti, and Chuck Giampa—gave Morales the decision, 115–113.

Morales was simply a more complete boxer. A better all-around technician.

"I knew boxing was the key," Morales said, "because he is so fast. He took a lot of punishment. We were prepared for his punching power and we knew he was quick, but, after the cut, I focused on punishing him. He was a very tough guy. I hit him with everything I had."

Roach was torn up about the loss, about how he had lost control of the camp. Roach is usually a soothing presence after a defeat. He is not an excuse-maker. But this duel felt like a lost opportunity. Maybe he hadn't groomed Pacquiao into as complete a pugilist as he needed to be, but Roach was also upset with himself for allowing the extracurricular bullshit to impact his charge. At the brawl's conclusion,

Roach cut off the gloves and waved them indignantly at Muhammad.

"I would have liked to use my gloves, but I had to go with what was in the contract," Pacquiao said. "I will fight him again anytime, anywhere."

Kevin Iole, the boxing writer, walked from the locker room to the press conference with Pacquiao. There was no mention of a weakened state because of the blood test. The excuse, some have suggested, would come later as Pacquiao searched for a valid reason for the loss.

BOTH MEN REMEMBER it well. Freddie and Manny were in a Las Vegas hospital. Pacquiao was getting his wound stitched up. They had experienced a devastating defeat. Roach was second-guessing everything. Pacquiao had become placid. Roach had never seen such a Zen-like attitude after a loss. It sort of bugged him.

Pacquiao told a disconsolate Roach, "There is a winner and a loser, and we lost tonight." Roach didn't like what he heard from Pacquiao. He wanted to see him breathe fire or seem more devastated, like the loss had cut him right to his soul. "I thought, 'Maybe he doesn't care that much,'" says Roach, "because I would never say that after I lost a fight." It took a few minutes for Roach to realize that this very moment would become a major part of Pacquiao's mythos. The theme? A Pacquiao defeat in anything brings a redoubling of effort. For Pacquiao, it was a turning point in the way he would now approach the sweet science. Most fighters privately make excuses. Pacquiao, a serious hypochondriac among other quirks, hadn't been 100 percent because he had his blood drawn, but he didn't complain about any phantom illness. The gloves were too cushiony for his tastes. The reporters had asked him about them, but he didn't discuss that with Roach, either. He didn't blame anyone or anything. *Was he a defeated man?* Roach always gives his fighters an out. ("I always say that I over-trained my fighter, or I did this or this wrong. It takes the pressure off. That is my job. To take the blame. One time I got fired because the fighter believed me, so you gotta be careful," Roach says.) Pacquiao wasn't looking for Roach to take the fall. As they sat there talking, it seemed like the failure was helping Pacquiao really re-examine himself. "It was a wake-up call," says Roach. The trainer didn't take Pacquiao back to the Wild Card; Pacquiao took Roach. He started working out right away. In closed-door sessions, they concentrated on Pacquiao's right hand. Pacquiao was a world champion, but he was far from the fighter he knew he could be. It was tantamount to Tiger Woods changing his swing after winning major titles. Pacquiao started working more diligently than ever. He seemed to crave inventing new ways to fight. He loves playing basketball because he revels in creating new moves as he plays. The loss to Morales revitalized him and made him dig deeper into his very soul.

"It's not a teacher-student thing as much as I show him a move, and he shows me how he'd like to execute it, and then we agree," Roach says. "When I let him interact, he's comfortable. He shows me the way he can adjust. When we can't work out the move, he'll say, 'Okay, let's erase that,' and we get rid of it. That way, there's no mistakes. With both of us working on the same goal together, he's become as smart as I am about boxing. It's scary how smart he is in there."

The Morales loss had a profound impact on Pacquiao's career, and it was the point in which the arc of his boxing life turned. It became one of those moments in a career in which the reaction to adversity lifts someone to greatness. It's like, in fictional sports movies such as *Rocky*, when Sylvester "Rocky Balboa" Stallone starts enthusiastically plodding through South Philly, eventually raising his arms to the sky. It wasn't quite so Hollywood, but the PacMan rededicated himself in the dingy confines of the Wild Card and trained now with a masochistic zeal.

"I studied why I lost that fight, and it made me into a much better fighter," recalls Pacquiao, who raptures about the Morales loss with something bordering on a discussion of the Resurrection. "My training became harder—we study our opponents; we coordinate our workouts." Pacquiao exudes enthusiasm. This might seem unusual to sports fans, but boxers don't always study their antagonists and create specific game plans for them. The thinking goes like this: Tinkering with one's style makes a fighter too wary. So most trainers will bring in sparring partners who fight in a similar style to the opponent and work from there. Roach's strategic approach keeps Pacquiao interested. The coordination between the two men has made a good boxer better. Instead of fighting as a straight-ahead puncher, a style susceptible to jabs, Pacquiao started weaving, counterpunching, and developing into an unpredictable tactician in the ring.

"We really started focusing on the right hand," says Roach, who gleefully calls Pacquiao's right "my baby."

WHILE PACQUIAO had experienced some legal issues with his manager, Murad Muhammad, Roach had helped guide him through the difficulty, and that cemented their bond even more. "I care about this kid, and I don't want to see him taken advantage of," says Roach. "Sometimes he asks me advice on his wife and kids and stuff like that; you know we have a good relationship, but we don't hang out too much outside of the Wild Card because I don't want to make the mistake of getting too close to him. I did that once in my life, and then I would tell my fighter to do something and he would kind of laugh it off, and I would say, 'I'm serious here, I'm not your friend, I'm your trainer.'"

To regain some confidence, Pacquiao took on Hector Velazquez for the vacant WBC International Super Featherweight title. On September 10, 2005, at the Staples Center in Los Angeles, he vanquished Velazquez in round six. Then, in one of the most anticipated fights of 2006, Pacquiao took on Erik Morales in a rematch on January 21 at the Thomas & Mack Center in Las Vegas. Besides the increasing pressures of fame (he would spend more than $40,000 to buy tickets for friends and family for his bout with Morales), Roach wanted to continue working with Pacquiao on some fundamental skills. "He was the greatest one-armed bandit in Las Vegas since the invention of the slot machine," says Bert Sugar. "Now he uses both hands. And not since Rocky Marciano has a fighter improved so much with every fight."

Roach and Pacquiao continued perfecting the right hand, as well as working on other skills: approaching his opponent

at various angles, his combinations, and moving after landing a combination. They did this behind closed doors. They
weren't really screwing around with cutesy nicknames like
Manila Ice, anymore, either.

MORALES II

MANNY PACQUIAO had never been so intense in his
workouts. Beating Morales in the rematch became an obsession. He arrived at the Wild Card on December 3 and stayed
away from his family during the holidays. He was developing
into a man who dreamed about his opponents. The Mexican
fighters had a reputation for heart, but it was their clever tactics that intrigued Pacquiao. Pacquiao told journalists that it
would be a "battle of brains, a fight to the end." Morales,
who answers to El Terrible, told people about Pacquiao,
"Sorry, but I'm just too superior." But the Mexican couldn't
help but respect him: "I respect both Barrera and Pacquiao as
sportsmen, but a little more respect goes to Pacquiao because
he gives everything in the ring, like I do."

In the second round, Morales was an effective counterpuncher, but Pacquiao's footwork was quicker. His punches
carried more risk because he was opening himself up. But
Morales couldn't seem to react to the perplexing hand and
foot speed fast enough.

Pacquiao, wearing white, threw a soft right jab and an
explosive left that hit Morales between the nose and the forehead. Morales, also in white, tripped backwards. In an
attempt to regain his senses, he shook his gloves in a frantic
shiver. Morales and Pacquiao exchanged blows and at the

end of the round, Pacquiao hit Morales with two solid rights. Pacquiao, tired, staggered to the corner.

In round three, Pacquiao started hitting the Mexican with right hooks, and then Morales came on with some good right jabs. Halfway through the round, Morales seemed to take control of the fight. Pacquiao looked a little tired. Pacquiao hit his gloves together, his sign that he would re-double his effort.

In the corner, Roach said, "Double jab then left hand to the body." He wanted Pacquiao to break down Morales's body before going for bombs to the Mexican's cranium. Pacquiao followed Roach's advice, but he looked fatigued. Morales jolted the Filipino's head backwards with a punch, but Pacquiao came back. Both men showed tremendous heart and respect—they would touch gloves after each accidental clashing of heads.

In considering Pacquiao's entire boxing career, this fight was proving that Pacquiao had developed an array of daunting punches. In the fourth through sixth rounds, both men were equally matched. Pacquiao was able to avoid many of Morales's punches because the Filipino would move laterally after throwing his combinations. The Mexican kept missing the target. But each fighter tried to break the other down and look for an opening to exploit. In the last twenty seconds of round six, Pacquiao threw combination after combination, and Morales stumbled back into the referee as the gong sounded. It looked as if one more punch and the Mexican would have gone down.

The fight looked over.

Then Morales played the aggressor in round seven, backing up Pacquiao into the ropes. Pacquiao didn't panic. After the first twenty seconds, he started going at Morales's body. Morales had a cut over his right eye and blood dripping from his nose. He looked glassy-eyed.

At the end of round nine, Morales backed up, dancing away from Pacquiao, who put his gloves together as if to say, "Let's fight." Morales looked beaten.

It was round ten.

With fifty-four seconds to go, Pacquiao threw a left hand at a tired Morales. The Mexican went down like a shot to the canvas. Morales took the standard eight count and got up with a second or two to spare.

When the fight resumed, Morales went down again almost immediately. It was the first TKO loss of Morales's career.

Buboy was crying.

His then promoter Shelly Finkel hugged Pacquiao.

The fans were going nutzoid.

When asked who he would fight next, Pacquiao said he would happily fight Morales again, that Barrera wanted a rematch, and that he would be more than pleased to take on Juan Manuel Marquez.

"I'm a fighter. So I fight in the ring."

AFTER THE FIGHT, Pacquiao returned to the Vagabond Inn (Room 120), a rundown motel next to the Wild Card where he routinely stays before his fights. He pulled up in a gray Porsche SUV and told the *Philippine Daily Inquirer* reporter, "I'm the storm across the Pacific." The reporter opined, "Pacquiao, with his screaming win, likewise succeeded in sending the timely message that the Pinoy can do a lot better than just clear out tables and wash dishes all over the world." But after Morales II, Pacquiao went back to his undisciplined ways. Pacquiao and Morales would conclude their trilogy at the end of the year, but Pacquiao hardly seemed focused on the fight. He spent days and nights shooting commercials, partying, and gambling in cockfighting arenas into the wee hours. Recah Trinidad, a Filipino journalist who has covered Pacquiao since his early days, says that Pacquiao has "two rival beings" caught inside his body.

MORALES III

MANNY PACQUIAO and Erik Morales would complete their trilogy on November 18, 2006, at the Thomas & Mack Center in Las Vegas.

Pacquiao would be favored in their third matchup. Morales struggled with weight again, and he seemed desperate to renew himself in any way possible. Morales had a high-tech training camp. He worked out in a plush Los Angeles gym, which made Roach visibly sick. (After that fight, Roach told me, "We did it the old-fashioned way—like a *Rocky* movie—and they did it 'correctly,' everything was precise, they had the fancy machinery and all that.") But Pacquiao was also undergoing a training renaissance of sorts. He was still getting hit on the stomach with a bamboo pole, but he was also searching for more advanced training methods to increase his edge.

To lend moral support, Morales had brought his father, José Morales, into his corner. The father had been missing from his son's corner only three times, including the second Pacquiao fight, and Erik had lost all three times. Make it four.

It was in the final seconds of round three.

Erik Morales sat on the canvas, arms around his knees, and stared at his corner. He stared at his father, José, who was urging him to get up. He stared as referee Vic Drakulich counted out the final seconds of his super featherweight match against Manny Pacquiao.

Morales never moved.

Morales was once labeled the successor to Julio Cesar Chavez. But he was dominated by Pacquiao, who had seemed to become quicker, smarter, and more powerful since their last meeting.

"It was futile," Morales said of the option of continuing the fight. "There was no point." Morales had gone down five times in just under four rounds against Pacquiao. "He was too fast, too strong. I did everything necessary in camp to win this fight, but it wasn't my night."

"I was faster and bigger than him," Pacquiao said. "He was coming to me, but he was not able to handle me." Everything had finally come together in the perfect storm: the right hand, the footwork, and the sheer power of his punches.

Pacquiao's fanbase was growing exponentially. The announced crowd of 18,276 was the second largest to watch a fight at Thomas & Mack. He had become the most recognizable Filipino in the world and every victory brought recognition and glory. At the end of the fight, Pacquiao, then twenty-seven, stood on the ropes and soaked it in.

Morales, thirty, contemplated retirement.

The fight hardly made American sports pages. A short *USA Today* article noted, "Though both fighters have only middling profiles in the U.S., each of their three pairings has been an international incident. Television sets from Manila to Mexico City were tuned in to the pay-per-view telecast of a fight pitting perhaps the Philippines' most famous person against one of the toughest fighters in Mexico's long line of famed brawlers. Thousands of Filipino fans traveled halfway across the world to Las Vegas for the fight, while thousands more came up from Mexico and Southern California to support Morales." It was a slugfest rivaling many of the best in boxing history, but boxing had become an afterthought, and no one in the United States cared.

Pacquiao was guaranteed $3 million for the match, much of which went to the IRS. Morales would make $2.75 million. Mexican fight fans, who demand action and valor in the ring, are difficult to please. But Pacquiao was starting to gain respect within the Mexican community, attracting fans south of the border that couldn't help but be excited every time the Filipino fought with a style they appreciated.

Besides dealing with the constant wrangling between Bob Arum, who edged himself in to promote Pacquiao, and Richard Schaefer of Golden Boy Promotions, who was saying that Pacquiao had signed a seven-year deal that began after the third Morales fight, Pacquiao had a lot of extracurricular activities to deal with: In February of 2006, Joanna Rose Bacosa, PacMan's alleged ex-girlfriend, surfaced and claimed that she had a son with the boxer. Later on, she filed a complaint at the Quezon City Prosecutor's Office citing Pacquiao's failure to provide child support. On March 21, Pacquiao was hospitalized due to stomach problems that were caused by his alleged "extra-curricular activities" . . . he allegedly also beat the crap out of a shoplifter in a General Santos grocery store. (Pacquiao denied it, saying that if he indeed "beat the guy," he would not have been able to get up for days.) He was linked with one of his movie co-stars, Ara Mina. The veracity of the report was questionable, but, of course, the Manila gossip scribes simply told him that he needed to be more cautious.

Pacquiao was not only busy in pool halls, cockfighting rings, and Manila nightclubs, but he was also running for Congress. It was an extraordinary source of amusement and worry to his countrymen. Pacquiao! In Congress! It actually wasn't the fact that the PacMan had an elementary school education, but rather the despair that he would become involved with an organization as corrupt and laughter-inducing as the Philippines Congress. Politics would tarnish him. Ask a Filipino in those days about Pacquiao's political ambitions, and they might even cry because they were so worried about his reputation. And Bob Arum, who had gone to the Philippines to support his boxer, worried about his life span. He saw Pacquiao's guns and the bulletproof SUVs. He heard about people getting shot and kidnapped. Arum loves politics, but this was something different. At that time, Pacquiao's desire to run made little sense to him.

Right before the election, Pacquiao fought little-known Jorge Solís. It was a poor performance. Pacquiao looked worn down. It took him eight rounds to knock out Solis. He hardly looked like the "Mexican Assassin." Had Pacquiao lost his focus again? Or did he thrive on the chaos?

BARRERA II

PACQUIAO'S NEXT BOUT would be a scratch against Marco Antonio Barrera. Pacquiao trained in the Philippines for his previous fight against the Mexican and won a unanimous decision. But without the constant guidance of Roach and the fewer distractions in Los Angeles, Pacquiao tended to veer off course. When he had the right people around him, Pacquiao was spookily focused, but when he didn't, his world seemed to go haywire. Pacquiao could just as easily veer from a disciplined path as drift into a vortex of all things dark. Back in Manila, the amount of savory attractions was limitless. Even his real friends had a difficult time seeing Pacquiao in the Philippines, a place of few secrets. (A resort owner once bragged to me that one of Pacquiao's children was conceived at his hotel. I stammered an *Oooookay*, and he said, "Seriously, I can show you the room!")

Barrera was a three-time world champion, but he was slowing down. He didn't look as sharp as when the two met in 2003. It was now October 6, 2007, at Las Vegas's Mandalay Bay. Pacquiao was brimming with confidence, as he entered the ring to defend his WBC International Super Featherweight championship. Marco Antonio Barrera, the Baby-Faced Assassin, wore red trunks. He clenched his teeth as he readied himself. As Michael Buffer (known for his signature phrase, "Let's get ready to ruuuuuuum-ble!), introduced the Filipino, Pacquiao smiled and laughed.

There had been a barrage of nasty exchanges between both camps in the lead-up to the fight.

Roach had said that Barrera's only chance was to "fight dirty." Roach had noticed that one of Pacquiao's only weaknesses was staying focused and sticking to his game plan after an opponent resorted to dirty tricks, like when he fought Agapito Sanchez in 2001 at San Francisco's Bill Graham Auditorium.

Tony Rivera, Barrera's cutman, who once worked for Roberto Duran, claimed that Barrera was so prepared for the fight that "we have three or four different plans. We're gonna see what Manny Pacquiao does. Whatever he's got, we're gonna counter."

Barrera cut in, saying, "We have A, B, and C."

As the fight began, Barrera tried to slow down the pace by dancing backwards. He circled. They had some flourishes, and Barrera wasn't exactly running away, but the defensive approach was the antithesis of a brawling Mexican fighter. He wanted to frustrate Pacquiao, and the Mexican eked out the second and third rounds on points.

In rounds five and six, the two men traded bombs. But Pacquiao couldn't quite knock down the elusively wary Barrera. It became obvious that Barrera was fighting to survive, not win.

In the eleventh round, Barrera began exchanging punches. Pacquiao, too quick, pummeled him good. He staggered the Mexican. They clenched. As the referee separated them, the Mexican, frustrated, retaliated with a vicious—and dirty—punch. The crowd booed. Pacquiao was in enormous pain, and the referee was forced to call a time out to let Pacquiao recover. The fight went to the end.

Of course, Pacquiao won in a unanimous decision.

Barrera thanked his family, sparmates, Golden Boy, and Dr. Ignacio Madrazo who in 1997 inserted tiny protective implants and removed abnormal blood vessels in his brain. The surgery nearly ended Barrera's boxing career prematurely, but tests showed there was no danger of brain damage if he continued to fight.

Barrera praised Pacquiao, but he also took it upon himself to introduce the Venezuelan Edwin Valero to the media. He predicted that Valero could beat Pacquiao. He also said that Pacquiao's power had declined since their 2003 meeting. After being beaten so soundly and barely surviving the eleventh round, the prideful Barrera had come across as an ungracious loser. The Filipino press was all over him.

But Barrera had a point. Pacquiao's punches didn't seem to have as much zip. His body was hurting. His movement wasn't quite so fluid. He couldn't get up on his toes. Going into his next fight against Juan Manuel Marquez, a stud, Pacquiao needed to get his body in tune.

WHETHER BOB ARUM is Pacquiao's most rational adviser is debatable, but he demanded a meeting. Training in the Philippines was obviously a mistake because there were like 2 billion distractions there. "I was not 100 percent focused, and I was not too excited by my performances in those two fights," Pacquiao, then twenty-nine, said. Pacquiao told Roach he was fighting at "50 percent" and felt "bored." But that was only a part of it. Arum summoned Pacquiao to, of all places, Las Vegas, home base for Top Rank. "I couldn't get him to concentrate on either the promotion or his training for Solis, and we held our breath as he trained overseas before Barrera," Arum told the *Los Angeles Times*. "That was ludicrous. It was with much trepidation that we sent him into that fight."

Arum had a two-hour lunch with the boxer. He told him he was on the verge of greatness. He noticed that Pacquiao's popularity was doubling with every fight. Arum, who was becoming yet another father figure to Pacquiao, slapped him down about his insatiable pursuit of the high-life. He didn't want him to be caught in a compromising situation, or get, you know, *killed*. Even for Pacquiao, the distractions were too many and unsettling.

"Some people advised me my performance was getting down, and I realized it was true," admitted Pacquiao.

Arum had a grand plan! Pacquiao had become so popular—through his fighting style, ring success, and backstory—that his 2008 fight schedule would pit the Filipino in a rematch with World Boxing Council super featherweight champion Juan Manuel Marquez, followed by WBC lightweight champion David Díaz in the summer. Arum was building toward megafights between Pacquiao and Ricky Hatton or even Oscar De La Hoya in the fall, the traditional season for the largest pay-per-view megafights. Arum, in his late seventies, was getting old. He was starting to think about his own legacy. He believed that Pacquiao, who seemed to be getting stronger and bigger, could be a crossover star. Arum knew that fighters with skill, charisma, and humility don't come along very often.

Arum laid down his cards. Training camp would be held at the Wild Card. When training in Los Angeles, he could not go on all-night gambling benders to the Commerce Casino to play poker. He had to curtail his pickup basketball games.

Pacquiao agreed and pretty much buckled down. He lived in a condo with a poster from his first fight with Marquez stuck to the wall for motivation. Roach taught him how to watch tape. ("You don't just look at just one fight," said Roach. "You find out what he does with every opponent.")

He started running a few times a week near the Griffith Observatory, a three-mile run with a very steep incline. Arum had spies to make sure that Pacquiao was keeping his nose clean.

"I go by results, and look at the results here," Arum said at the time. "He's in unbelievable shape. I've never seen him in this kind of shape. He's incredibly fit and focused, and I'm sure you'll see the best Manny Pacquiao you're going to see. At his best, he's a nonstop machine."

Said Pacquiao: "I want to be known beyond the Philippines as a great fighter. I realized no one can help me in the ring but me. I feel confident, with no doubt, about the good performances that are coming this year, and that starts now. You'll see a big difference between this fight with Marquez and the first one."

JUAN MANUEL MARQUEZ II

IT HAD BEEN FOUR YEARS since Pacquiao's first controversial fight with Juan Manuel Marquez, and he would take on the Mexican again on March 15, 2008, at Mandalay Bay. Marquez, thirty-four, trained like a fiend. Every weekend he would run up the Nevado de Toluca volcano, a 15,354-feet mountain. Marquez had called his first Pacquiao meet-up the most frustrating of his career, and he was set to prove himself. He had lost only one of thirteen fights, winning all four of his championships, scoring four knockouts and upsetting countryman Marco Antonio Barrera in a WBC title fight in 2007. He credited the high altitude training at Toluca with his success. Marquez's camp atop Toluca consisted of a squat concrete building without heat or electricity. Marquez and his training partners would spend sleepless nights shivering under layers of street clothes and as many as three blankets, then rise before the dawn to run, as a green Pathfinder—the SUV's headlights casting an eerie glow on the rugged, rock-strewn trails—followed them. Marquez would run in a down ski jacket, sweat pants, and a wool cap, carrying four-pound weights in each of his gloved hands. "We're always saying that between the humility and the suffering is where you're going to go forward," said his fitness trainer. "When you run alone in the mountains, under adverse conditions, you're training your mind. Because your mind can say *no mas*. And your legs can keep going."

"I don't know why people think he's the Mexican killer," Marquez said. "He [Pacquiao] didn't beat me. This fight is for me, my fans, and the Mexican people." The fight was called "Unfinished Business" because four years earlier in their first meeting it had been declared a draw. If anything, Marquez, serious, was at the height of his boxing powers. He wanted to destroy the man who had become the "Mexicutioner," a nickname Pacquiao deplored.

Pacquiao's second fight against Marquez was a thriller between two evenly matched fighters. Pacquiao was stunned in round two. He kept throwing a straight left, and in round three he deceptively altered its arc by throwing a short left hook that dropped Marquez. But for much of the fight, Marquez controlled the ring. Pacquiao came in close to Marquez with dangerous bursts of punches. But Marquez survived the third and rebounded to win the majority of the remaining rounds. It was an extremely close fight. It went down to a decision. It was a split one with Pacquiao eking out the win—a great victory against a brilliant fighter in Marquez, and yet almost everyone, including the Associated Press, ESPN, Yahoo!, Reuters, the *Philippine Daily Inquirer*, and Filipino Sports analysts Ronnie Nathanielsz and Recah Trinidad had it going to Marquez. Pacquiao won the vacant *Ring* magazine junior lightweight world title, but the magazine editors didn't believe he won the fight.

Pacquiao wasn't delusional.

The training camp had been a disaster. He made weight at 129.5 pounds, but he ballooned to 149 on fight day. He felt hog fat and sluggish, and he found Marquez's counterpunching style difficult to handle. Pacquiao had had shoulder problems, too, during camp. Alex Ariza, Roach's new conditioning coach at that time, was asked to take a look at Pacquiao's wing. Ariza would work on Pacquiao's shoulder every night at 7 p.m. Pacquiao started feeling better, and the two men became friends. Ariza got in the Filipino's ear about nutrition and how he needed to have a highly prepared diet plan going into fights, if he was going to continue to go up in weight classes. Starving and bingeing would not work. Ariza also developed a plan, with Roach, on how to better strengthen and add muscle tone to the Filipino through stretching and fitness drills.

PACQUIAO TOOK ON David Díaz, a flat-nosed brawler, on June 28, 2008.

Pacquiao dominated the fight. He cut Díaz's nose in the second round, and a few rounds later he opened a gash above the right eye of Díaz. It was a bloodfest. The cut was bad enough to prompt the referee to have the doctor look at it twice during the fight. Pacquiao hurt Díaz with an upper-cut in round eight, and in the ninth round, a jab followed by a left hand that Díaz never saw coming. It sent him down face first to the canvas, and the referee jumped in to stop the action. Pacquiao had become the only Asian fighter to win four major titles in four weight classes.

Pacquiao had created enormous momentum for himself.

While the Mexican fighters were his toughest competitors, it would be his next two fights—against Oscar De La Hoya and Ricky Hatton—that would bring international acclaim.

The public believed Pacquiao would be no match for Oscar De La Hoya, the handsome Golden Boy. Going up so far in his weight class seemed suicidal. Besides the additional weight, De La Hoya was five inches taller. But De La Hoya's camp knew better than to take Pacquiao lightly.

After all, Schaefer saw what happened to Barrera five years ago in San Antonio.

"I'm pretty worried about this fight, actually," Schaefer commented. "Manny doesn't just win. He hurts people."

9

MANNY IS A HYPOCHONDRIAC

IT IS DIFFICULT to see Manny Pacquiao's eyes as his head is encased in glittering gold headgear to protect the champ's brain. He wears matching gloves and groin protector. His cartoonish road runner–like feet, which are difficult to follow with the naked eye, are clad in red Nikes. He wears a blue "Just Do It" MP T-shirt. He crosses himself. It is something he does with regularity.

Bam-bam-ba-ba ba, he sings while he spars.

Mike Dallas Jr., a young pro with quick hands, is his sparring partner. He can't seem to keep up with Manny's speedy footwork, which creates odd angles for the African American fighter. But Pacquiao lets Dallas hit his body, which would hurt a lesser man. "Thanks for the massage," Pacquiao says. Pacquiao slides away easily, and Dallas swings wildly at the air. Even when Dallas gets in tight, he can't seem to connect with Pacquiao's evaporating body. Dallas, five foot nine, seems mesmerized. Then he nearly hits the PacMan below the belt. Pacquiao laughs, but he is clearly irritated.

Round one of the sparring session is over. Pacquiao strides to his corner.

"He hit me low."

"No he didn't, Manny," says Alex Ariza. "It was here, above your hip." The acoustics in the gym are amazing, every ear attuned to Pacquiao's words.

"It was low."

"Manny, we can watch the videotape. I saw it."

Everyone sort of ignores the back and forth. Manny Pacquiao laughs at his own expense, but not much. Manny, everyone whispers, is a hypochondriac. Even if Dallas hit him a little low, no one wants to feed into Pacquiao's neurosis, which crops up frequently in training camp. Pacquiao gets back into the center of the ring.

The kid starts hitting him a little low again.

About two nano seconds later, Pacquiao's feet glide over the canvas and then suddenly dig into it as he throws a flurry of punches, precisely timed. Pacquiao nails Dallas in the solar plexus with a straight left. Dallas stumbles backwards and grimaces as a wheezing sound emanates from his headgear.

Manny, laughing, dances back to his corner.

Ba-ba-ba-ba-ba-ba.

He is greeted with a torrent of guffaws. Laughing with Manny seems to be a prerequisite of working for him. "A smiling Manny is a good thing," people mutter. It is early in a training camp, and the sparring partner didn't have too much experience, couldn't really grasp Manny's seasoned boxing calculus. So Manny taught the kid a lesson with the punch. "It hurt, right here, never felt that kind of pain, it made me trip over my feet, headgear came over my eyes, still hurts," says Dallas. Two blondes, rough around the edges, spray-on tans, knee-high boots, and skirts hiked beyond decent, try to get into the gym, which is closed for Manny's workout. "Manny, take a picture with us!" Get out of here, someone barks. Manny wants to please people—to a fault everyone says—but it is a bad idea to interrupt Manny's workouts, even thirty days outside a fight, because Manny wants to control the mood, and the mood needs to be joyous, eyes on him clowning around.

Twenty minutes later, Dallas still can't seem to catch his breath. "He's goes at such a fast pace, and he is so quick," he gasps. He seems worried that something might be broken or shattered.

Everyone is good. Manny Pacquiao, the hypochondriac, is left unscathed. He feels great. He is smiling. His positive outlook will reverberate around the world. Everyone, from the twenty people in the gym, to the millions of Filipinos following his every move through the papers or television or on the Internet will know that the PacMan is okay, smiling, and now, so are they.

Manny Pacquiao has become the anti-embodiment of modern sports. Sure, he has a small contract with Nike, and they have produced a hip line of Pacquiao athletic apparel, but gossipers whisper that he was completely had in the negotiations, but Pacquiao isn't very corporate. Partly, it is the state of boxing, a virtually ignored sport, but it is also him. He isn't easy to define. It helps that he is one of the most recognizable Filipinos in the United States and pretty much anywhere else in the world. But in a game in which one loose punch can end a career, Pacquiao can be anxious and irritable in private. Freddie Roach gives his sparring men $1,000 if they knock Pacquiao to the canvas, which adds to the pervasive tension in the ring. But there is more to it, a deeper-seated worry that has nothing to do with boxing's risks. "Very Third World," Alex Ariza tells me. "Suspicious of vaccinations, that sort of thing." The people around him understand his quirk because most of them share in the paranoia about the modern world. They don't exactly want it broadcast, and they also don't want to pamper him. ("If he misses one meal, his life almost ends," laughs Roach.) Everybody makes a living off Manny Pacquiao, and everyone seems to love him. Get him in a hypochondriac funk, and Manny isn't so fun to be around. A happy Manny means a pleasant person outside of the gym, and a focused and ferocious masher in it.

Talking with Filipinos about Manny Pacquiao can feel like entering a cult. Pacquiao arrived in America when not many Americans could identify a famous Filipino, save Imelda Marcos or Corey Aquino. He might have shared the stereotypical notion of the quiet, sweet, and tireless work ethic of his brethren, an almost anti-celebrity, but instead he became a one-man chamber of commerce. A commonly accepted stereotype was that Filipinos were invisible voices: good in choirs, poor soloists. They didn't really stand up for themselves; they were a gentle, inconsequential tribe. As Pacquiao continued winning and whipping his countrymen into a frenzy, the parades through the streets of Manila grew by the hundreds of thousands. Filipinos started following him with the sort of fanaticism usually reserved for religious idols. Pacquiao's popularity continued to rise exponentially outside the archipelago, which incited Filipinos to become even more Pacquiao crazy. Secretary of State Hilary Clinton said she was a Pacquiao fan, and other world leaders and celebrities nodded in admiration. To Filipinos, he emerged as their voice. *Time* magazine, which has followed Pacquiao more diligently than any other Western news organization, calls him a "demigod." But a boxer as a national idol comes with risk: He can be killed in the ring, and boxing's reputation is hardly pristine. And athletic fanaticism is followed by "haters." Inevitably, as Pacquiao became popular, more people started knocking him. They wrote irritating things about him. They accused him of outrages. They said he was over-rated. Filipinos had the right to take him to task, but outsiders? To Filipinos, this was like attacking a family member.

"I WANTED MANNY to become a priest," says his mother, Dionisia. "Among my six children, he is the most religious. When he was just a boy, he used to accompany me to early dawn masses. At the age of twelve, Manny could easily carry a thirty-liter container filled with coconut wine in each hand. My neighbors would comment on how strong Manny seemed. He was not an ordinary kid." She is wiry, like her son, and looks much younger than sixtysomething. At her sixtieth birthday party, held at a General Santos convention center, she wore five expensive gowns, including one for greeting her guests, and another for dancing. (Everyone says she is addicted to dancing.) She wore a Rolex (a gift from Jinkee) and carried a Louis Vuitton handbag. She sent a special invitation to Imelda. But she also invited *anyone* else who wanted to come. "I asked Manny for this, and I'm so happy he gave it," she said of the lavish affair. Despite frequent trips to Manila, and an occasional journey to the United States, she prefers General Santos to any spot on earth. "It is really true that there's no place like home," she says. Son and mother are practically inseparable, and they talk on the phone when he is away from her.

She is only five years removed from abject poverty, but she is a proud woman who doesn't live her life to be intimidated by anyone. She will work a crowd, making them laugh about her foibles. She willingly tells the story of her son without any sanctimony, just in a matter-of-fact way. It is his mother who lets him continue to fight, and there is much speculation in the press about when she wants him to stop. Is it one more fight? Or three? She wanted him to quit at age thirty, but he keeps going back to her and asking for another one.

MANY PEOPLE HAD started centering their lives around him.

Freddie Roach became the second most popular man in the Philippines. It wasn't simply an occupation for Roach. He obsessed about it. He opened his gym at 6 a.m., and he was often closing it down at 8 p.m. If he was training fighters, he might not have time for lunch, so in the late afternoon he would take a quick break and eat almonds and dried peas out of a plastic container brought from home. When he wasn't at the Wild Card, he was probably coming or going to a fight. Many people thought he worked too hard, but there was a time clock going off in his head. It was thrilling when everything went right. He was able to see the strengths and weaknesses of fighters, his own, and their opponents, and vocalize a winning strategy. When a trainer would give advice to a fighter that Freddie thought was nonsense, he would make a sly comment, "That guy knows next to nothing and his second knows less." But he was more than just a trainer in the corner creating winning schemes; he tended to micromanage the entire gym. Two Los Angeles Police Department officers created a boxing program to help juvenile delinquents. "Freddie, is it okay for the cops to watch Manny train?" "Sure, gotta give back." Plus, the female detective is good looking, and no one wants her to leave. *Freddie! Freddie! Freddie!* Everyone wants Freddie. One of the gym hands takes a call; he holds the receiver and whispers to me: "A multimillionaire wants a Wild Card T-shirt and he wants to talk to Freddie about it. Unfuckingbelievable."

While he had grown to tolerate the attention from fans and the media, Roach didn't really care about the adulation, and if someone looked a little lost he would come up and say, "Everything all right?" There are a million melodramas in boxing, from the promoter who shortchanged a fighter, to trainers trying to steal a good prospect, and they all eventually pass through the Wild Card. So many different characters have trained in the gym or brought their fighters there to work out, spar, or just get noticed that a hundred different slights and good tidings were walking into the place everyday. There were plenty of people who had wronged Freddie, too, but he tended to forgive the ignorant and simply kill them with kindness ("I can get information from them that way," he says).

On a lazy day in training camp, as the greatest fighter of the modern generation trains in his gym, Freddie Roach looks over Pacquiao with fatherly pride. This is what Roach loves most of all: improving his fighter, teaching him more tricks.

Some white guy with a Mohawk who talked his way into the gym stands in a sort of awe as Manny jokes with his friends in Visyan and does basketball poses in the ring, acting like he is shooting a jumper. It's 2:02 p.m. Manny nods his head from side-to-side to warm up his neck. He moves his arms like a windmill. He does hip rotations like an exotic dancer. Then ankle stretches and shoulder rolls. "How ya doin', all right?" Roach asks Pacquiao. The sparring partners are out of earshot. "Got three here, but one guy won't last, I'll make sure of that." At 2:17, Manny shadowboxes for five minutes. Then Ariza massages his shoulders. Manny sits down. Ariza intensely massages the champ for ten minutes. The PacMan has to be loose. Pacquiao puts his arms into different positions, extending them backwards. By 2:23, he is putting on his gold groin protector. Buboy puts Vaseline on his face. Pacquiao looks placid as Buboy tells a regular photographer in the gym, "No photo, no flash. Go outside." Everyone laughs. To Pacquiao, his training camp needs to feel like family, like people working together. His work ethic is impressive. (Bill Caplan spent time with Sugar Ray Robinson and says that Robinson is the only true comparison to Pacquiao's prodigious work in the gym.)

I get a tap on the shoulder.

"We need some help."

They are writing a thank-you note to a Wild Card employee.

It reads, in really shaky handwriting, "Your doing a great job, Thanks."

"Can you make it neater? Make it nicer."

My handwriting is messy, but I do my best, and I fix the grammatical mistake and six guys are looking over my shoulder, studying me, seriouslike, similar to the way I study their punches, and someone says, "Pretty good," and they all nod. I say, you needed to fix the "your," and they nod again, sagely, not really knowing what I am talking about.

And now to the sparring.

As Pacquiao is hit, he says, "Up, up, up."

Pacquiao starts slow. He makes his combinations but doesn't duck away. He gets hit. He invites punches into his body. He is trying to find his rhythm.

By the third sparring round, he says, "C'mon boy, c'mon boy."

By round four he is going 80 percent.

"Are you okay?" he asks Dallas.

Dallas is so winded that he doesn't really respond. Dallas steps on Pacquiao's foot.

"Good strategy," says Pacquiao, and everyone cracks up.

By 3:01 p.m., his sparring gloves are off, and he puts on green gloves and hits the heavy bag for four minutes. No one talks; it is quiet, like a church. Roach is trying to give Pacquiao light work today. Just ten days ago, the PacMan had gone fifteen rounds on the mitts with no rest. They always worry about Pacquiao peaking too early.

Freddie tells Buboy, "Right, right, left hook." Buboy talks to Pacquiao about drawing his left out a little longer and then does a throat slash. Pacquiao just stares. By 3:23, his gloves are off. His shirt is dripping with sweat. They worry about him getting a cold, and his team gets him a new shirt. "In training, you do two or three combinations, in the fight one or two," he says. He gets on the speedbag by 3:25 and beats it senseless for ten minutes. ("He has the fastest hands I have ever seen," says boxing historian Bert Sugar.) Buboy and Alex then get to work on removing his hand tape. Pacquiao playfully hits a member of the entourage in slow motion. He checks his abs at 3:29 p.m., and then a child comes into the Wild Card. "Daddy, daddy!" she screams at the guy with a Mohawk. Pacquiao smiles at the little girl.

After being dried off again, he starts jumping rope by 3:38. Pacquiao's calves are enormous. Roach tells me "all Filipinos have them." I ask a Filipino friend about this dubious observation, and he just laughs at my stupidity for falling for Roach's joke. At 3:50 p.m., the jump roping ends. *Right, right, left hook.* He concentrates on moving laterally. The fundamentals of balance are something he obsesses about improving. (Emanuel Steward, the hall of fame trainer, told me that good balance can make a good fighter great, and Europeans have done so well in the pugilistic arts lately because they work on developing this crucial asset. "That's why they are dominating fighters, because they teach balance in the European countries.") Pacquiao's balance is superb, and he is constantly working on it. Because of his balance, Pacquiao is able to do six-punch combinations, followed by four-punch combos, followed by six combinations. His punch output is astounding because he is always in a position to hit. Roach settles down and relaxes. Pacquiao starts shadowboxing. He changes shirts again.

Pacquiao and Ariza start doing sit-ups, or what the coach calls plyometrics: They do sit-ups using a two-pound medicine ball. Pacquiao twists his torso and starts throwing it at Ariza.

"That's four," says Ariza.

"That's five."

"That's four!"

"Fuck you!" The gym explodes in laughter.

He does one-handed pushups on balls and strengthens his neck by putting a ten-pound weight on his head. They then go back to doing the sit-ups with the medicine ball, "More shoulders, Manny."

Ariza came to the Wild Card gym after his client, Diego Corrales, died in a motorcycle accident. Living in Las Vegas, Ariza wanted to apply the scientific techniques he learned at San Diego State and work with professional athletes. He had some boxing experience, and he knew Roach listened to new ideas. So he sent his résumé to the Wild Card. Roach had wanted to integrate modern nutritional techniques into his training. Although Roach believes in old style methods (sex before a fight is verboten, although every fighter in the gym rolls his eyes on that edict), he also feels that athletes have improved in other sports through nutritional means and modern training techniques. Roach is a firm believer in road-work, sparring, and boxing workouts that have been going on since Jack Dempsey, but his fiancée at one time was a world class runner, and he understands that boxing is behind the times. Ariza quickly earned Roach's trust: Roach's fight-ers were making weight, and the varied workouts—track work accentuated with footwork drills—and gradually increasing plyometric work were paying dividends as the Wild Card fighters seemed just a little stronger and mentally more engaged.

Working with Pacquiao wasn't always easy. The Filipino had essentially done the same workout for fifteen years, but he was a willing student. The constant bamboo pole beating became something for the cameras more than a regular part of the routine. In sparring, Roach would give him tips, like getting him to move both ways around the ring, and they would study film. They were creating a more strategic boxer, but he wasn't training like a modern Premier League soccer player or an NFL wide receiver. Ariza simply added some drills to Pacquiao's regimen, specifically quickness drills on the track, many of which were aimed at opening up his hips to develop more power. At first, Pacquiao didn't feel quite right. New muscles were emerging, and he didn't feel as quick, which was Pacquiao's forte. Ariza actually wanted to scrap the program, as he didn't want to go down in history as the guy who destroyed Pacquiao. But Roach told him to keep at it. He realized that if they were going to go up in weight, Pacquiao would have to develop the strength of someone larger in frame. Boxers tend to drop down in weight class to use their bodies' frames to dominate smaller men. While this is a technique that has been around since the days of bare-knuckle fighting, it can also tend to weaken bigger men as they starve themselves.

Roach was attempting to do something radical. Using boxing-specific strength training, he wanted to slowly build Pacquiao's punching power and weight. Roach secretly believed that Pacquiao could fight welterweights, an almost twenty-five-pound increase from his professional debut. Going up ten pounds is not uncommon because as a fighter ages it is difficult to keep off weight, but twenty-five pounds was unheard of. It was a unique challenge and one that carried great risk for Pacquiao's health. A big-punching, natural welterweight would have a significant and potentially lethal advantage. Just packing on muscle doesn't help a boxer because it is a sport that relies on speed as much as punching power, which emanates from coordination and flexibility. Pacquiao was an excellent subject for this experimentation. He had been undernourished and seemed to go through a late growth spurt, almost like he was still growing into his body. Pacquiao's short attention span was also beneficial. As much as Pacquiao wanted things exactly the same in his personal life, he was easily bored and liked when Freddie came up with new ideas. Pacquiao was no dummy, either. He knew enough NBA and Major League Baseball players to realize that boxers weren't always taking advantage of new training methods. While Ariza's new regime initially made him uncomfortable, sparring partners were dropping to the canvas one by one. "For a such a small guy, he has tremendous power," his sparring partners would mumble.

The talk inevitably turns to steroids again. It is a subject that Ariza actually likes to chat about. While Pacquiao has never tested positive for any performance-enhancing drugs, there is an emerging skepticism about his ability to get bigger and faster. The type of people who write bitterly about the famous on the Internet started calling Pacquiao "Pacroid" and the like. This is an affront to Ariza. "Steroids? I take the allegations as a compliment. Misery loves company. They can't imagine what he does in the gym, the hard work and sacrifice. It's not about motivating him, it's about slowing him down. He is like a horse at the gate, just wanting to push through." Ariza hears the whispers, and it bothers him because he sees his boss as a man of honor: "He refuses to take Advil or Motrin. He is such a person of honor. Someone hits him low; Manny is told to hit back at the same range—Manny refuses to do it. Manny won't fight you dirty."

The workouts are intense and other fighters—some belt holders like Julio Cesar Chavez Jr.—come to watch for inspiration. Ariza is always arguing with the Filipino about rest days. Manny pushes himself to the limit, secretly running on Sundays when Ariza begs him to let his body recover. "What amazes me?" asks Ariza. "The consistency of his workload, his level of intensity—100 percent. He is still getting better. His quickness and times are faster. He runs a 4.5 forty. Still getting faster. I think he is a late bloomer. And outside the ring, he is learning movie lines, playing chess. He is an intelligent man and getting more intelligent. I think it helps him inside the ring."

After his morning run, usually between three and ten miles (or a track workout), and his work at the Wild Card, Manny likes to play basketball. Freddie has a rule that he can't play a month before fight time. It is a difficult rule to abide by because Pacquiao loves the game. Why? (If he could be anyone he would be George Foreman. "Not only because it would give me an opportunity to win a world title in an eighth weight division, but . . . I would be big enough to play power forward in the NBA!" he jokes.)

Basketball games with Manny's entourage are the worst kept secret in Los Angeles's Filipino community. He rents out a local high school, and the gym is packed, even though sometimes he shows up hours late because he has some other commitments (meeting with the MTV Cribs people, maybe, or shopping at the Grove) or abiding to his intense nap schedule. But the people will wait for hours just to get a glimpse of the diminutive boxer playing basketball while his handlers worry themselves sick that he might twist an ankle.

IT IS 7:13 A.M. in Los Angeles, and Manny Pacquiao is on a public high school track. The sky has turned from dawn into an overcast Southern California day. There are palm trees in the distance, and the low hum of traffic on Highway 10 is starting to turn into a low roar. Pacquiao is three weeks away from a fight. He wears a red tracksuit, black gloves, and a black hat. It's fifty-two degrees and chilly. The rains have stopped. The track is dry. His entourage, straggling on to the infield, one holding Manny's thermos of tea, another holding a mat, others talking with each other, while others do calisthenics and yawn. The Filipino television reporter is in a neon green tracksuit and running around the track. A whistle blows. "C'mon Manny!" yells Ariza. He runs a 2:04 warm-up lap around the oval. A member of his entourage runs with him for fifty yards, but he can't keep up. Another member runs with Manny's dog, a Jack Russell terrier named PacMan, which barks frantically whenever it isn't near its master. (The revealing of the dog's name was given its own segment on the Filipino national news.) Manny is always on his toes in the ring, but when he is running on the track, he is a heel striker. To develop even more stamina and core strength in the ring, he exaggerates his arm movements and runs ramrod straight. "Hold that stomach tight! Arms up high! That's it! Perfect!" A couple dozen Hispanic students, clinging to a chain-link fence, are watching Manny go through his paces. An administrator is pleading with them to get to class. "We love you, Manny!" a kid yells. Pacquiao holds up his hand in recognition, grimaces, and carries on, alternating between jogging at a crisp pace, and running backwards. He is nursing a severe shin splint on his left leg. Ariza worries about it, frustrated that Manny won't rest it for a few days. "If he is in the fight, and his leg is killing him in the third round, then he will have wished he rested it," says Ariza, who says Pacquiao is showing some concern, too.

Ariza structures a light workout this morning and will avoid any quick footwork drills. He has placed cones on the grassy infield, and Manny does sprints. He does the grape vine quickly and then jogs back to the first cone. "Turn the corner! C'mon!"

He returns to the track and quickens his pace ("Stretch it, Manny! Stretch it!") to a 1:52, but he doesn't appear to be running all out. With Ariza guiding him, Pacquiao alternates between the track and the patchy grass field. He wants him to run backwards as much as possible to help with the shin splint. When he was a kid, back in Mindanao, Pacquiao—like anyone without money—would walk for miles because he couldn't afford the couple of centavos for a bus. There is a theory that Pacquiao, running in his bare feet, became such a freak of endurance in the ring because of his constant running. When he was kid, he was known to run up to ten miles a day. Now he wears his own brand of Nike shoes.

At 7:47 a.m., the person whose primary responsibility in life is holding the mat is yawning and not paying attention to his duty. Someone yells at him. *Manny is ready to do his sit-ups!* The man does his impersonation of a sprint while wrestling with the mat, gets close to Manny, and puts the mat down. Other members of the entourage avoid him. Embarrassing incompetence. He won't be sleeping at the front of Manny's bed tonight. Manny does various crunches: regular sit-ups, knees to chest, twisting. It is a familiar routine for him. A member of the entourage holds his feet. Manny does this all without speaking. People describe him as childlike and someone who needs constant attention, but in these moments he has the intensity and concentration of a stalking lion.

At 7:58 a.m., Manny begins to pray for a minute or so.

He crosses himself.

Buboy takes his gloves. The person responsible for the thermos rushes over with Manny's tea.

To the chagrin of the high school administrator, six or seven kids have been hanging out waiting for the workout to finish. "C'mon, get to class!" But they refuse. Buboy is handed cell phones and acts as the photographer. A young girl sheepishly hands Pacquiao a piece of paper, which he signs. With the students, he smiles. The administrator really wants the kids to go to class, and an LAPD officer is closing the gates to the school. Alex Ariza is talking about how Manny had the best sparring session of the camp yesterday. "Ten rounds. Really sharp. Manny wants to go another ten. Freddie was very happy." Manny hobbles to his black Escalade and gets into the passenger seat. He is off to eat some breakfast and to put ice and heat on his left leg. Ariza says his other concern, Manny's tender right hand is healed, but it is getting closer and closer to fight night, and Ariza is starting to get nervous. Manny isn't smiling as much as everyone would like.

Everyone around him relies on his fluctuating, temperamental moods. They are all in deep. Their very future is predicated on the outcome of his fights.

10

GOING GLOBAL

IT'S 12:27 P.M., and the grand opening of the Manny Pacquiao Merchandise Store was supposed to start twenty-seven minutes ago. Filipinos are gathering around the store, which is located below the Wild Card Gym. This is Pacquiao's foray into branding himself. In the sickly looking strip mall, the store's entrance is blocked by blue, red, and green tape. Winchell Campos, beleaguered, is in the back of the place. He has handwritten a sign for everyone to come back at 4 p.m., and a rumor starts buzzing among the Filipinos that Manny Pacquiao might show up. *He's not vacationing in Mexico!* they whisper. Looking over the store, hardly any of the boxes unpacked, Campos, who until recently referred to himself as "Pacquiao's biographer" and is now selling Manny Pacquiao T-shirts, lamps, and posters, says, "This is a way to help Manny after he retires."

The haphazard strategy of turning Pacquiao into a global pitchman and a global figure has been in the works since the late 2000s. In the Philippines, his image is plastered on billboards that advertise gin (with his mother), motorcycles, Victornix watches, and Nike products. One of his advisers told me that Jollibee, a popular Filipino fast food chain, rejected the notion of using Pacquiao in any of its campaigns because the PacMan tends to show up in the gossip pages too much. But in August 2010, Sony Philippines named Pacquiao as its brand ambassador. His popularity might sell products—two platinum records, he has starred in seven movies—in the Philippines, but until 2010 Pacquiao has done a terrible job of capitalizing on his fame globally. Part of the problem is that Pacquiao has an edict, which he repeats to his entourage: "Bring me a deal; you'll get 15 percent." This keeps the entourage motivated, but it also creates a free-for-all, especially since his associates know that Pacquiao prefers "cash up front." Business advisers who have tried to guide him estimate that Manny Pacquiao has probably given up 70 percent of his potential endorsement deals because he always wants his money first. "What's a royalty?" he asks. A lucrative cologne deal was shot down because the money wasn't upfront. Pacquiao has apparently produced his own cologne, M7. In the Pacquiao store, Campos flourishes a bottle of it as a Filipina sniffs it with pleasure.

Lucrative speaking engagements never happen because organizations insist on cutting him a check *after* he talks. Actual corporations, especially outside the Philippines, have wanted to sign him as a celebrity endorser but cannot seem to figure out what a few of his American educated advisers call—with a straight face—his "business model." People around him are reluctant to hand him a contract because they worry he will sign it, take the money, and forget about his obligations. There is an internal struggle between some of Manny's more legitimate representatives and the entourage.

Some call the conflict the MBAs versus the Entourage. *Who's winning?* In my observation, Manny's MBAs, some of whom are graduates from America's finest universities, are no match for the entourage. Pacquiao's old friends from General Santos City contact executives at major corporations, such as Procter & Gamble, to strike a deal. Marketing managers across the United States field calls from people whose primary dialect is Visyan, who could have literally been picking coconuts days earlier, and who sleep at the foot of the Pac-Man's bed. They would like to schedule meetings with the executives to work out a deal. Most of the corporations have stopped fielding the annoying and perplexing calls. Who represents Pacquiao? I once asked a legitimate Hollywood agent who has worked with him. "No one—and I mean no one—legitimate." Even when one of his more well-regarded representatives strikes a deal, there comes a great amount of hand wringing because the entourage controls Pacquiao's schedule. Around the gym, I hear that they didn't really know the name Phil Knight, Nike's chairman, and they blew off a meeting with one of the most powerful men in sports. (A representative from Nike denies the meeting didn't take place.)

Besides blowing off meetings, the way the money is handled presents challenges. An executive from a large video game manufacturer insisted on giving Pacquiao a check directly because he didn't trust the entourage; he showed up one day unannounced at Pacquiao's apartment and handed him $50,000. Pacquiao looked confused. And yet, strangely, Pacquiao's screwy life actually feeds the public interest in him. He could be a *Harvard Business Review* case study in counter-intuitive marketing. Unlike a neatly packaged star, like Roger Federer or even—before his fall—Tiger Woods, the PacMan's image is so ridiculously uncrafted that he stands apart from all the IMG- or Ari Fleischer–guided sports celebrity robots.

Pacquiao's unpredictability has produced even more interest in him, they say. Considering the blind loyalty of his fans, there might be something to this. They wear T-shirts emblazoned with his image or the statement "Freddie Knows" or "Buboy Knows," like these men are apostles. Any negative mention of the National Fist in an online article, and comment pages will fill up with the vitriol of his supporters. Picking up on the obsession of his fans, the *Los Angeles Times*, and other publications, try and cover Pacquiao as much as reasonable because Web traffic spikes on stories about the PacMan: Even cash-strapped AOL sent a reporter to the Philippines to write about Pacquiao. Pacquiao's fan base is always there—online and off—for him. Before Pacquiao fought Miguel Cotto, a Twitter message was sent out that Pacquiao and Roach would make a public appearance and talk about the upcoming fight. The event would be held in Hollywood at the Montalban, a Nike-sponsored hipster store. One out of every four Filipino Americans make their home in Southern California, numbering more than 1 million. But they are not the only fans of the fighter. Hours before the event started, a line with pretty women, tough-looking fight fans, and hipsters stretched around the block, all wanting to catch a glimpse of the Filipino. He's cool.

Despite the passion around the fighter, he misses endorsement opportunities all the time. His haphazard marketing and his crazy-as-hell money management style worry the people who care about him. They worry he will eventually go broke. Following a fight, he gets 40 percent of the purse after he pays everyone. His wife gets 30 percent of his money. She has a boutique business in which she buys expensive handbags and resells them, but she has a reputation for more orthodox spending and saving habits. "If he earns, say, P50,000, he gets to keep P20 and the rest goes to me," his wife told Recah Trinidad, the journalist. "We could not split it down the middle. I have an entire household and the kids to maintain. Besides, Manny has a very expensive lifestyle." When Pacquiao gets paid, there often comes a torrent of financial irresponsibility. He uses hand signals to dictate cash transactions. It is not unusual for someone in his group to carry a briefcase full, it is rumored, of $100,000 in cash. The money flows to different people, from street people with sob stories to more legitimate business deals. Most people say he won't go broke because his riches go so far in the Philippines, and yet . . . Pacquiao's myriad number of businesses, from pool halls to convenience stores, to his gifts of Rolex watches, to clearing friends' gambling debts, real estate, roosters, M-16s, hospital beds, a cinderblock business, apartments, houses, condos, and God-knows-what-else quickly drain his net worth.

CAN A FIVE FOOT SIX Filipino boxer with a weak command of the English language become an American star?

After Floyd Mayweather Jr., Pacquiao's rival, won a big fight in 2010, he sat in the pressroom talking with reporters. Mayweather was guaranteed $22.5 million. He was still undefeated. It was a special night.

But he was upset that so many Americans favor Pacquiao, especially because Mayweather had "the USA on my back." He had represented the United States in the 1996 Olympics, earning a bronze medal. But Mayweather's notion of fandom in the age of globalization might be dated. Of course, Americans tend to cheer for Americans, but with the foreign integration of the NBA and Major League Baseball, a foreigner, if sold correctly, can easily become a star in the United States.

The NBA, which was considered a purely American game almost a decade ago, is now populated with foreign talent: Pau Gasol (from Spain) for the Lakers, Yao Ming (from China) for the Houston Rockets, and Steve Nash (okay, he's Canadian) of the Phoenix Suns are all legitimate stars. And just a few years ago, Englishman David Beckham, one of the most popular athletes of the modern era, joined the Los Angeles Galaxy of Major League Soccer. He was part of one of the most focused marketing efforts in recent memory, helped by his celebrity wife, model-like looks, likeability, and an ability to speak English. Beckham, a "lifestyle icon," was too often out of the lineup because of injuries and other commitments, helped sell hundreds of thousands of Adidas products (he was on a nationally aired Adidas commercial with American football star Reggie Bush), his own cologne (Instinct, "a masculine, sexy, exceptional fragrance"), and other products—such as Vodaphone and Giorgio Armani. Despite his weak effort on the field, Beckham now has tremendous name recognition in the United States.

Pacquiao would like to do something similar, but he can't seem to pull it off. Pacquiao has charisma and public likeability—magazines and newspapers send correspondents to cover him because so many readers are passionate about him. He trains in Los Angeles, owns a Beverly Hills mansion, is trained by an American, hobnobs with American singers, actors, and sports stars, and has become a novelty with a younger demographic who view him as a mix between Ali, Bruce Lee, and Robin Hood. At the very least, marketers who would like to tap into the tens of millions of Southeast Asians in the United States should view the PacMan as an ideal spokesperson. He is comfortable in front of the camera. He likes to perform. In photo shoots, he immediately becomes model-like, hitting every mark and facial expression with ease. Jerry Jones, the owner of the Dallas Cowboys, is a fan and one of the best sports marketers in the world. He helped make the NFL Cowboys into the most recognizable American football team. He was able to convince cash-strapped taxpayers to build a $1.2 billion domed stadium, which seats from 80,000 to 111,000. Cowboys Stadium also has a retractable ceiling that protects against rain. Jones is particularly proud of the stadium's major feature, a monstrous, high-definition screen known as the "Jerry-Tron," which is believed to be the largest in the world. Jones is a huge Pacquiao fan and helped bring him to Cowboys Stadium for a bout. He told me that Pacquiao has an "aura" and compared him to one of his former star players, Michael Irvin. "Michael has an aura. He had a way to create energy. Manny has that. I know what it is. It's taking a talent and maximizing that talent and walking the walk. That's what he is. He walks in and has that aura."

TOP ECHELON ATHLETES usually have a team of American marketing and brand geniuses guiding their every step.

Pacquiao's image management is sort of handled by Michael Koncz, another beleaguered individual whose responsibilities seem to mainly include keeping journalists away from his boss and watching over Pacquiao's money. When anyone wants cash, Pacquiao immediately agrees; Koncz, meanwhile, says no to people asking for ridiculous sums because, for example, they gamble too much. Everyone seems to scheme and try to work around Koncz, who protects his boss with a zeal that gets everyone upset. It doesn't always make sense, that's for sure. Photographers in the middle of a photo shoot will be told in no uncertain terms that it "might end right now" for no apparent reason. Reporters from the largest news organizations will beg for ten minutes of Pacquiao's time but never get their phone calls returned. Even Pacquiao's promoters have a difficult time working through the labyrinth and often just give up. Usually celebrities hire expert wranglers to create a "media strategy," but the iron wall that Koncz erects around his boss has, ironically enough, seemed to engender more interest in the fighter.

Just look at the popular ABC television program, *Nightline*. Even after being discouraged to visit General Santos, *Nightline* producers hungered for a Pacquiao story. The millions of Americans that watch the show were treated to . . . Pacquiao napping.

A reporter and crew were flown to General Santos, but they were barely greeted with a "Hello." The frustrated reporter, not really knowing the ways of Pacquiao, ended up interviewing Koncz, who said Pacquiao's ambitions were "not a ploy to get publicity or anything." The reporter then looked at the camera and told America that Pacquiao had kept her waiting six hours . . . then nine. When Pacquiao appeared, she nicely introduced herself, and Pacquiao sort of ignored her as several million Americans watched. Pacquiao left his house in his armored Hummer, and the reporter breathlessly said, "We are desperately trying to keep up with Manny's car, and we have no idea where we're going!"

It was to . . . a basketball court. She was treated to Pacquiao playing a four-hour game of hoops and ignoring her some more.

His lack of interest in fame seems to make him more intriguing and more famous. But this type of attitude has its limits.

THERE IS A GREATER reason than his boxing brilliance for all of the attention. Pacquiao's global appeal doesn't come from selling soap or shoes but from what he sees as his greater purpose: his fight against poverty. His bid for a congressional seat in 2007 failed, but in the spring of 2010 interest around Pacquiao's political mission seemed to congeal. "The people have rallied behind him and feel like they're a part of him, because they can see his talent, his dedication, his grace and his class," Lennox Lewis, the former heavyweight champion told *Time*. "The grip he holds over the Philippines is similar to Nelson Mandela's influence in South Africa. I can surely see Manny becoming the Philippine president one day." When this quote was repeated, Filipinos would laugh. They admired Pacquiao, but they also thought of him as a child. No one wanted him to run for office, and most people thought he would lose. But his campaign created a groundswell of interest among nonsports fans who saw him as a crusader for the world's impoverished. The *Philippine Daily Inquirer* talked about Pacquiao's increasing fame. "Whether it is a banker in Hong Kong or an airline employee in Jakarta or a taxi driver in Singapore . . . " and encouraged the wacky idea of "boxing diplomacy" in which the Philippines president when traveling abroad "can invite Pacquiao to conduct a boxing clinic—as a way to engage the youth (and the children of host presidents), but also as a means to get front-page media attention. . . . It will attract the kind of media mileage that presidential visits from developing countries cannot even hope to achieve. And it will be good for our image."

Pacquiao's bouts and endorsement deals have brought him millions. In 2009, Forbes ranked him number fifty-seven among celebrity earners with pay of $40 million, but there is a lot of precedent for boxers blowing through their money and becoming punch lines and tragic figures, the most famous being American fighter Joe Louis. Louis was the heavyweight boxing champion from 1937 to 1949, but he ran into financial trouble and ended up greeting tourists at the Caesars Palace hotel in Las Vegas. More recently, Alexis Arguello, the great Nicaraguan boxer and politician, who in November 2008 was elected mayor of Managua, allegedly committed suicide on July 1, 2009. Rolando Navarette, a world-class featherweight from GenSan, spent three years in a U.S. prison for sexual assault, and he now sells fish to scrape by. And then there is Mike Tyson who has blown through tens of millions of dollars. Pacquiao is aware of these stories. In boxing gyms, penniless ex-pugilists are everywhere. There are also down-and-out characters trying to get something from Pacquiao, an easy mark because of his generosity to anyone with a sob story. Pacquiao sees his ability to provide charity as a direct gift from God. Doing it quietly and with class is as important as the money.

One day, a seven-foot-tall homeless man was outside the Wild Card. He used to play professional basketball in the Philippines. Great hook shot. Unstoppable. When he lived in the Philippines, he was rich. He had maids, cooks, and a chauffeur. Pacquiao walked by him. Pacquiao wasn't going to pity the man and let him lose face. The man asked Pacquiao for money. Pacquiao gave a hand signal and someone from the entourage handed him one hundred dollars. Pacquiao told him to buy some shoes, sounding like a kindly priest. Pacquiao knows his Filipino basketball history. He recognized the man, but he didn't want to bring him any shame. The next day, Pacquiao saw him again. The man had shoes, but there is no way they cost one hundred dollars. "Where's my change?" Pacquiao smiled.

PACQUIAO FINDS INSPIRATION and the miracle of life in many places. He draws strength from his good fortune, especially since Filipinos tend to have a hell of a lot of bad luck. They find glory in persevering, and surviving. Anecdote in point: Pacquiao knows well and finds great pride in the story of Domingo Lucas—a flyweight contender known as Pretty Boy Lucas. Lucas was a hard-luck Filipino who fought for but never won a world title. He went the distance with

Ricardo Lopez in 1992 but lost in a unanimous decision. In 1995, Pretty Boy was fighting in Tokyo where he suffered a hematoma after exchanging head blows with Chang Jae Kwon. His skull was opened to relieve the pressure. The miracle of titanium had yet to gain favor in the Japanese medical system, so a good old-fashioned metal plate was placed on the left side of his skull. To this day, if you see Lucas, the left side of his head is as flat as a runway and quite prominent. He used to tend to a pig farm in Bulcan, which is north of Manila. Pacquiao only sees the dignity in his life. He is a hero to Pacquiao.

ONE EVENING, Jimmy Kimmel, the comedian, sends a stretch Hummer limo ("Gets eight miles to the gallon, tops," says the driver) for Pacquiao and some friends. Kimmel likes boxers, and he particularly gets a kick out of Pacquiao. After a light workout at the Wild Card, Pacquiao and his crew take a ride to Kimmel's studio at the El Capitan Theatre. It's the boxer's second appearance on ABC's *The Jimmy Kimmel Show*. Pacquiao is at ease. He has his own program back in the Philippines, a sketch comedy show called *Show Me Da Manny*, which is a play on one of Manny's favorite phrases, "Show me the money," but the nationally broadcast Kimmel show is his chance to test out his comedy chops and singing skills in the United States. His Los Angeles–based voice coach, who has traveled with him in the Philippines and seems unbelievably frustrated that she can't give him a proper lesson ("We grab fifteen minutes here or there, in his car, while he is eating," she moans), implores him to warm up his tongue, and he starts rolling his R's, sounding like a crazed cricket. After visiting his dressing room, where his aunt has come to see him before the show, the PacMan goes through a few warm-ups with Kimmel's studio band.

"Nothing's gonna change my love for you . . . "

A guy holds up old-fashioned cue cards so Manny won't miss any lyrics of the George Benson tune.

His voice coach, who Manny met at church, asks, "Is that key okay for you? That was C, right?" The band members nod. There seems to be an enormous amount of sincerity and seriousness around Pacquiao's musical number. The place is empty. The stage manager goes through the routine. "First you will be up here, and you will be interviewed, then Jimmy says, 'We'll be right back,' and then you will sing."

Manny thanks the band ("Not all celebrities are that nice, believe me," says one stagehand) and, practice complete, goes back to his dressing room to chill. The El Capitan is filling up with people. There is a party going on in the Green Room, where drinks are served, and the whole place feels like a hip cocktail lounge with young Hollywood types wearing sunglasses inside and just hanging around socializing while the regular folks from Kansas and Manila in the studio audience are getting pumped up by an enthusiastic bald guy who manically gives out T-shirts and DVDs and tells the audience to "put your hands together!"

Pacquiao is content to go back to his dressing room and relax for an hour. It is a little cold. Someone is sent to turn up the heat ASAP. Pacquiao drinks lukewarm SmartWater (in the limo ride over, there was a tub of ice filled with bottled water; I had offered him one, and the entourage went ballistic—*Don't you know ice cold water hurts his throat!?*)

and goes over his lyrics. Koncz sets up his dinner, which is takeout from Nat's Thai, fluffs his rice, and cuts his employer's meat. There is an odd dynamic in the room, but everyone seems to think the procedure is normal: If someone from the show wants something, they talk to Koncz, who simply repeats the request *in English* to Manny who then tells Koncz his answer, in English, who in turn says the same thing to the show representative. No one even blinks at the nontranslation translation.

It is 6:11 p.m. Makeup has been applied. The sound man mic's the champion. His Nike representative has given him a handsewn red letterman's jacket, which has been dubbed "The Destroyer Jacket." There is a red "17" on the front: "That is my birthday, December 17." His children's names are on the back. Everyone looks to him as the leader, but he doesn't really talk very much. His English, while halting, is always much more smooth around his friends. When he is asked a question by an interviewer, he seems to desperately look for words, like he is trying to appear intelligent. He has now practiced his song about ten times since leaving the Wild Card. The vocal coach tells him to put his right hand in the air when he sings. His security guy tells him someone is giving him a DVD player so he can watch fights on his private plane. Manny doesn't really look up. He doesn't notice his environment, including the photographs of different guests—P. Diddy, Matt Damon—on the mauve walls. He is texting on his cell phone and checking basketball scores. Duke versus Maryland is on the big-screen television in the room. "Breathe from the stomach," says the voice coach. Someone in his entourage says,

"Manny, can you mention your upcoming concert in Waikiki?" Manny gives an acid look.

It's 6:48 p.m. Manny's brother, Bobby, a good boxer himself, is in the room. He wears black Lacoste tennis shoes and jokes with people. Their aunt, who wears a purple jacket and seems in shock to be in the room and about ready to see her nephew on television, is ushered to her seat in the audience. Manny swigs more SmartWater and burps. Someone is talking about Manny being on *Good Morning America*. Pacquiao's voice coach asks, "Chamomile tea?" "I don't know. . . ." Manny is hesitant. He has to be careful what he puts into his body. "No, it's okay. It's what I drink," she says slowly, mothering him. "Okay." Someone from the entourage falls asleep in the makeup room, and another person takes a plastic bag and pops it, waking up the dozer. Everyone laughs. Great times. "Celtics 104, Charlotte 80," says Manny, reciting an NBA score. He is a Celtics fan. "Kevin Garnett made him into one," a security guard from Boston says.

It is 7:04. Voice coach: "No sugar, just chamomile tea." Manny is very reluctant, but he takes a sip. "Did you like the tea?" "Yes, it's nice," he says, sweetly. Actually, it seems unimaginable that he is such a ferocious boxer. The room is now warm. A couple people from the entourage discuss watches, one person saying, "I'm going to get my Rolex soon from the boss." A producer comes in and lays out what Kimmel will ask him so the interview will go smoothly. (Soon afterward, I am called out of the room and told that the details of the conversation can't be repeated because of "trade secrets." The producer, who at first I think is breaking my balls, says, "Can I trust you, buddy? *Can I?*")

It's 7:15 p.m. Everyone watches Kimmel go through his opening monologue on the big-screen television. The cheering can be heard in the Green Room when Kimmel mentions Pacquiao, who winks confidently. Kimmel jokes that he "has a voice of an angel." But Pacquiao isn't laughing. His voice coach pushes his head to the side to a worrisome degree, she massages him. He does various mouth stretching exercises. He listens to her because she has sung on an AT&T and American Airlines commercial. He makes noises, "Little higher," she says, "Get that tongue turning, turning." Ethan Hawke is interviewed. ("Who's that?" asks Manny.) A show photographer comes in. They show Manny shadowboxing. Finally, Manny comes out on stage. He wears black shoes, jeans, an oxford shirt, and the red Nike jacket. The crowd chants, "Man-ny! Man-ny!" Kimmel asks him about how many people live in his apartment. "Ten guys, up from eight," jokes Manny. Kimmel asks about Mayweather's allegations of steroids use. Even though Kimmel sets it up easily, Manny flubs the question, and his response is incoherent. "I am open to fight anyone," he says, finally. Kimmel tells Manny he should go on *American Idol* and sing, and if the judges don't like him, he can "beat the crap out of them." The crowd laughs. They talk about his political ambitions. They show a clip from one of his movies, which Kimmel calls, "Probably the best movie ever." It shows Pacquiao fighting a giant crab. "That should be your next fight."

Pacquiao then sings. The crowd loves the campiness of it. His high-pitched voice crackles. The American hipsters sip cocktails in the Green Room. They are the cool crowd. They sarcastically guffaw about how he should cut an album. Ho! ho! ha! ha!

After the performance, back in his dressing room, Pacquiao is beating himself up. He says, apologetically, "I was thinking about basketball."

"No, no, that was great!" says his voice coach. "You blew it out of the water!"

Manny signs some boxing shoes for the president of ABC.

In the Hummer back to the gym, several autograph seekers chase the car on foot. One guy is particularly insistent.

Manny Pacquiao says, "Okay, stop. Roll down the window."

The autograph seeker says, "I have been waiting for four hours. It's cold out here." Manny signs the photograph.

The car continues. Manny is conferring with his voice coach. "They played it faster than usual, but you kept up." Outwardly, she is proud. She slaps him on the knee.

To the people in the limo, Manny announces, "Good interview with Jimmy Kimmel, huh?" He sounds a bit insecure. Everyone says he was "amazing," "great," "fantastic." A couple people don't say anything. This is all so normal, and yet foreign. Someone had asked him to be on the *Jay Leno Show*, too, but the entourage, unfamiliar with Leno, had turned the show down, not really fathoming that it might help Pacquiao have an even wider American audience. Someone tells Manny he looked relaxed, and the producers want him back on the show, even though they are a little pissed that Pacquiao never signed the standard ABC television release from his first appearance last year and they can't give him the nine hundred dollars they owe him. The

Hummer driver has a hell of a time backing the twenty-seater into the Wild Card's parking lot after the nearly one-mile drive. As soon as Pacquiao gets out of the Hummer, a crowd gathers around him. Some people shove gloves in his face. He ignores them. He is tired. "Manny! Manny!" shouts a little Latina girl, who looks about seven. She is doing laundry at the Laundromat near the gym. "Will you take my picture with my mama?" Gently, he puts his hand on her black hair, pats her head, and nods. A picture is taken, and then Pacquiao turns from the crowd, escaping the fray, into the Hollywood night.

11

THE GOLDEN BOY AND THE HITMAN

AFTER THE REFEREE'S instructions and a lukewarm touching of gloves, the crowd bellowed, "MAN-NY! MAN-NY!" There was a hell of a lot of yelling from people who couldn't seem to control themselves.

Oscar De La Hoya, an old hand now at thirty-five, went to the middle of the ring. It was December 6, 2008. While in great shape, De La Hoya carried himself tightly. His hands were raised like an old-fashioned bare-knuckler. He wore burgundy shorts and matching Cleto Reyes gloves, and black boxing shoes. Pacquiao, a significant underdog, bounced around like an over-amped rabbit. They were both so pumped with adrenaline they didn't really hit each other for a good while.

De La Hoya looked like he was in a foul mood. Pacquiao was intent on jabbing with his right, but he would also sneak in a straight right, and that made the Golden Boy tentative: He was gravely concerned about Pacquiao's left, the Filipino's stronger hand. Pacquiao bobbed and weaved. Jabbing, De La Hoya concluded, was futile. As a kid, he would wake up at 4:30 a.m. and do his roadwork, but that seemed so long ago.

The way he ambled in the ring tonight, it looked like he wore the heavy boots of a construction worker with tired legs. With about fifty seconds left in round one, De La Hoya caught Pacquiao with a left hook to the body. It was a good shot and Pacquiao seemed to trip over his own feet. But that was like a lone grammatical mistake in a prize-winning novel. De La Hoya's best punches mostly creased the Vegas air.

There were some calls of "Os-car, Os-car," but the enthusiasm of the Filipinos—whether the action was good or bad—sucked the sound out of the cheers for the Mexican American. De La Hoya had been good for a long time. Growing up in East Los Angeles, he had been a kid who ran away from fights. His mother, who habitually puffed on Kent cigarettes, believed in her boy, who tended to cry a lot. He came from a family of fighters, and he turned to boxing as a matter of course. Despite his peace-loving nature, he proved to be a dynamic boxer. When De La Hoya was seventeen, his mother died of cancer. Before she passed away, at age thirty-nine, Cecilia told her son to win the Olympic gold, which he did at the 1992 games. He was a sure-bet star: handsome and bilingual with a whispery voice that made women swoon. He lived a fast life, admitting—in his autobiography—that he lost $350,000 at the craps table one night (estimating $2 million wasted in gambling losses before going cold turkey) and would sometimes go to strip clubs to *talk* with women because "sex was always available to me." Eventually, he gave up gambling, married, and settled down with a Puerto Rican pop star.

Before the fight against Pacquiao, De La Hoya seemed more passionate about his promotions company, Golden

Boy, golf, and his kids than beating the crap out of someone, but he trained in Big Bear, in the mountains outside of Los Angeles, with as much intensity as he was capable. Going into the megafight, De La Hoya, ever studious, saw flaws to exploit, and he believed he had a chance to vanquish the spritely Filipino. But watching the tape didn't prepare him for Pacquiao in the flesh, and it certainly didn't reveal how much Pacquiao's ring mechanics had improved in his last eight bouts. Just two years ago, he was using a predictable double-jab followed by a straight left, constantly going forward and hoping his speed would overwhelm his opponents. After the Morales loss, he had never stopped learning new techniques. He mixed up his repertoire, sometimes leading with the left. He was now out-thinking and out-quicking his opponents. His combinations, sometimes four, sometimes six, changed every round. His head moved. He came toward his opponents at angles. "Without science and tactics, the pugilist's nob soon becomes a mere dummy in the hands of his opponent," wrote the grand master of boxing writing Pierce Egan. He still tended to follow his combinations by backing straight up, but by anyone's definition, Pacquiao was now a man of science.

In the ring, De La Hoya's punches still had snap, but they couldn't seem to find Pacquiao's torso or cranium. The Mexican Assassin struck De La Hoya in the nose several times. The Golden Boy's face was starting to swell. The bell gonged.

Pacquiao sat on the stool. He looked rather fresh. "Very good," said Roach, who felt a surge of confidence. De La Hoya has no legs, he is hesitant, he is shot, Roach thought.

"Keep boxing. It's important that you keep your back off the ropes," he said.

Pacquiao had trained for the fight with incredible zeal, and the Filipino's confidence was growing with De La Hoya's every lackluster punch.

In the opposite corner, De La Hoya sat heavily on his stool. He needed clear and concise answers from his corner in how to outbox Pacquiao. Nacho Beristain, his trainer, philosophized that Pacquiao was quite susceptible. "All he can do is a straight hand or a hook, and he doesn't know what to do, he trips. Lively, lively. Assert yourself, assert your jab." The Golden Boy's cornermen rubbed Vaseline on the boxer's face.

After a minute of listening to these musings, De La Hoya, puzzled, slowly marched to the middle of the ring. His head was still an inviting target that seemed to be getting larger, like a balloon. And another reason for trepidation: He couldn't seem to move his head. Of course, De La Hoya had a size and weight advantage. Most people thought the fight would ruin Pacquiao, who had not fought in a division above lightweight (135 pounds), and here he was going against a natural welterweight. De La Hoya had come into the night as a two-to-one favorite, and that brought a hush to the gamblers who had bet the favorite. He would undoubtedly put his superior size to work in round two.

De La Hoya moved forward and jabbed but still couldn't find the target. Pacquiao punched through De La Hoya's shield of gloves. There was a rather sizeable and throbbing welt under De La Hoya's left eye as the Golden Boy, protecting his face, bent down. His height advantage vanished.

Beristain: "Don't look for him without throwing punches. Jab, jab, jab, and throw."

Roach: "Keep boxing him. He might start taking chances. Keep boxing smart. In and out, side to side."

In round three, Pacquiao hit and ran, never winding up his punches. De La Hoya, who had one of the best left hands in boxing, refused to use it. Desperate, De La Hoya looked to land a power punch with his right, but he couldn't really land anything as Pacquiao pinned him in the corner. De La Hoya's body and boxing brain were definitely not in sync. More than any other sport, boxers can seem to lose their skill set in a nanosecond, but De La Hoya possessed such formidable skill that he was able to cover up his deficiencies at least for awhile. Which De La Hoya was here tonight?

Against Sugar Shane Mosley in 2003, De La Hoya had problems making weight and celebrated by gorging himself with suspicious oysters from an East Los Angeles restaurant, an unorthodox place to dine on shellfish before a championship bout. He claimed to have eaten a bad one, which weakened him before the fight. The ashen De La Hoya thought he could outpace the speedy Mosley and was simply beaten to the punch as they each tore into one another that night. He lost. Then it was Felix Sturm (won in a unanimous decision), Bernard Hopkins (loss via a ninth round knockout), Ricardo Mayorga (victory with a TKO in the sixth). Then he hired Roach for his megafight against Floyd Mayweather Jr., who De La Hoya called "a very insecure person." Forty-eight hours before the fight, Oscar seemed weak from losing so many pounds to make weight—he was barely audible when I asked him a question at the prefight press conference. He fought smarter against Mayweather by sticking behind his jab to neutralize the shorter opponent's speed. But De La Hoya's stamina betrayed him late as he got outworked. "I didn't feel any power when he hit me," De La Hoya says. "I don't know how he knocked out Ricky Hatton. I really don't." Mayweather is a brilliant defensive fighter, and De La Hoya found it difficult to find him, even limiting his height advantage by crouching for many of the later rounds, a strategy that befuddled Roach. ("My back was killing me," De La Hoya explained to me.) He lost in a split decision, but felt like he should have won. "He wasn't all that great." De La Hoya bounced back with a lopsided decision versus journeyman Steve Forbes, but Forbes, a career lightweight who lacked much of a punch, left De La Hoya's face more bruised and battered than it had ever been after a fight.

About Pacquiao, he said, "I know he's a strong fighter, and I have to figure out a way to pull the trigger. . . . I have to find a way to increase my speed. I have quite a task in front of me. We have to figure out quick how we're going to neutralize him. It's going to be an explosive fight. My pride, and Manny's pride."

"Twenty years from now, thirty, forty years, I want my name to be at the top level of boxing history," Pacquiao said. Roach had devised a strategy to pull off the upset. Having worked in De La Hoya's corner, Roach knew Oscar's tendencies intimately. "Manny has to take the jab away from Oscar, get inside the jab, fight at short range," said Roach. "Oscar is a distance fighter. He has long arms. I don't think it's huge. But it's our biggest problem. And it's no secret we're going to attack the body first and break him down." Pacquiao claimed his usual weight when not training was 155, so the jump in weight class wasn't bothering him. But that was gamesmanship. In truth, he has a difficult time keeping on the pounds.

In round four, De La Hoya strode toward Pacquiao, who wore red shorts and red shoes. De La Hoya would land a right hand, barely glancing Pacquiao's head, but Pacquiao would nail him with a less-friendly uppercut and a two-shot combination. "MAN-NY! MAN-NY!" As round five came along, there was an inevitability sinking into the contest. Pacquiao had more skill and tactics than De La Hoya, the most skillful and tactically sound fighter of his era. By cutting off Pacquiao's left side, he started moving the PacMan in a counterclockwise direction, a smart strategy to force the southpaw off his left pivot foot. Pacquiao simply hit him with his right hand. By my count, he hit him nineteen straight times at one point midway through the round. A few years after the fight, De La Hoya told me, "I was a shell of who I was years ago." He also said Pacquiao was "one dimensional," which seemed far-fetched to anyone at ringside who watched the variety of punches and movement from the Filipino.

Before the fight was over, they were comparing Pacquiao to Roberto Duran, who had carried his weight to higher weight classes, from 135 pounds to handing Sugar Ray Leonard his first loss in 1980. Duran almost beat Marvin Hagler for a middleweight title, too. Unlike Duran, Pacquiao looked even faster at the heavier weights. The name Henry Armstrong was also bandied about. Armstrong, ranked the second greatest fighter of the last eighty years, won boxing championships in three weight divisions (at a time when there were fewer weight divisions than today) and held three world championships at the same time.

Between the rounds, Beristain asked: "Are you okay? Do you want to go on?" De La Hoya seemed to shrivel. The Golden Boy's legs fluttered under his trainer's hands as they were rubbed.

Styles make fights, goes the old saying, and in rounds six and seven it was evident that Pacquiao's style was overwhelming De La Hoya, who seemed to age ten years in twenty minutes. His wife, Millie, was screaming to stop the fight. De La Hoya had to hold on to the top rope to keep his balance, and all three judges scored the round 10–8 for Pacquiao, despite there being no knockdown. De La Hoya, once a star, was watching his universe disappear. On the press tour, he had watched as people came out to see the Filipino. "I've been in the streets of this land, and the word I get is that Pacquiao means so much not just because of the excitement of his boxing but what he is as a man."

Roach told his pupil to keep turning De La Hoya. Pacquiao controlled the center of the ring. An amazing variety of punches sprung from Pacquiao. He hit De La Hoya with a left cross that stunned the Golden Boy. He pressed him into the corner. De La Hoya's face was wearing out Pacquiao's gloves. De La Hoya didn't punch back. His left eye was closed. He hit De La Hoya with fifty power punches.

De La Hoya stopped the fight. He retired from the ring. Roach went to him, his old boss, to see if he was all right. "I'm okay, I just don't have it any more."

"Oscar was my idol, and, actually, he is still my idol, but I always believed that I would win this fight," said Pacquiao.

Pacquiao—too young, too fast, too strong—kissed his gloves and looked to the heavens, which was the ceiling of the MGM Grand.

SUGAR RAY LEONARD and Tommy Hearns came together to talk. They have lived their rivalry for twenty-nine years now. Theirs was a classic fight, a matchup of dissimilar styles—elegance versus strength. Leonard and Hearns bring a serious longing for the best modern fighters to actually face each other. Back in the early 1980s, the nation cared about two men pummeling each other. Each man had earned a welterweight (141 to 147 pounds) championship belt—Leonard from the WBC, Hearns from the WBA—so their storied fight unified the belts. They fought in a special 2,500-seat arena constructed on the grounds of Caesars Palace casino in Las Vegas. The media covered it with gusto. The fight grossed $36 million, at the time the richest single sporting event in history. Says Leonard, "Fights were highly anticipated, and [boxing] personalities were superstars. So even if you weren't a boxing fan, per se, you had heard their names." Their fight defined them. After a seesaw battle, Leonard charged out of his corner in the fourteenth round, racing over to tag Hearns with a huge left hook before the Hit Man could step out of his path. Soon enough, the third man in the ring stopped the fight. Hearns, who had been ahead on points with all three judges at that moment, looked on incredulously. Angelo Dundee, Leonard's manager, said, "Tommy Hearns was out of it. He didn't know where he was." Hearns' trainer and manager, Emanuel Steward, acknowledged that the referee had made the right decision.

Leonard, Hearns, Roberto Duran, and Marvin Hagler were all excellent boxers and fought each other, producing what boxing writers like to call "epic" fights. Because of a detached retina, Leonard retired a short time after his Hearns fight, but unretired several times before taking on the Hit Man again in 1989. It was ruled a draw, but everyone, including Leonard, believe Hearns won that one. All four men—the four kings—made people care. Rivalries, the best competing against the best, create interest in sports, but boxing doesn't regularly pit the best against each other, especially in the pay-per-view era. Boxers are reluctant to blemish their precious records because it can hurt future paydays. Pacquiao was willing to take on all challengers. Fans respected his courage.

While they still have the grace of gazelles, Leonard, fifty-four, and Hearns, fifty-one, look like in-shape business executives. The years haven't seemed to tarnish them. Hearns, with the waist of a boa constrictor, is unusually tall (six foot one) for his weight class. "Tommy Hearns is a freak of nature for a welterweight, big, strong," says Leonard, deadpan. "No one can beat Tommy Hearns—except me." Hearns slurs his words a little: "The fight with Ray and I was so huge. No one knew how we were going to be. Our fight is talked about for decades and decades. Everywhere I go, people still ask me about it. I am proud to know Ray Leonard. He brought the best out of me, and I brought the best out of him."

Leonard and Hearns are now friends. Says Leonard, admiringly, "He took everything from me, physically, spiritually."

With his victory over De La Hoya, Pacquiao's name had started surfacing as one of the best boxers of his generation, maybe ever.

IN ROUND ONE of the much-hyped junior welterweight fight, both men were on their toes. Ricky "the Hitman" Hatton, pale as the moon, came forward, scrambling to throw off the PacMan's rhythm. Pacquiao commenced hugging, and the Hitman returned the embrace with some good liver shots. Pacquiao was annoyed. Hatton was beating Pacquiao to the punch for the first twenty-five seconds. It was May 2, 2009.

Joe Calzaghe and Hatton had become the stars of British boxing. The English can rightfully lay claim to their homeland being the birthplace of the sport. The Ancient Greeks didn't mind punching each other, but the modern concept of boxing started around 1719 when James Figg, the "Father of Boxing," was acclaimed as Britain's first national champion. This notable achievement is widely acknowledged as marking the official beginning of boxing in the modern era. In a time when cities were becoming overcrowded, business disputes would be settled by rolling up one's sleeves and duking it out. Boxing was a less lethal alternative to swordsmanship. The Queensberry Rules, published in 1867, are still the primary guidelines for the sport. There is a lot of history and pride in British boxers. Hatton had many fans, who would travel many miles to watch his fights, drink copious amounts of booze and sing bawdy songs in his honor.

Coming into the bout, Hatton had a healthy polish. Hatton, thirty, would not have age as an excuse. In the parlor game that is boxing analysis, Pacquiao's win over De La Hoya had been impressive, but it was being devalued because of the Golden Boy's declining skills. (Hatton called De La Hoya, his promoter, a "punching bag" in that fight.) Pacquiao-Hatton was described as a pick 'em. The *Sports Illustrated* writer covering the fight said, "Put a gun to my head, and I'm taking Pacquiao. While I think both have the punching power to win by KO, I have a feeling this one goes to a decision."

Ricky Hatton had lounged ringside at the De La Hoya–Pacquiao match. He studied how Pacquiao dismantled the Golden Boy. "My goal was to fight the winner, and Pacquiao has proved that he's the best fighter in the sport," said Hatton. The Englishman noticed how Pacquiao threw a combination and then went under and out of range. He thought he could exploit it. It looked, well, predictable. Outside of the strategy talk and fight hype, the two men actually liked each other's company, not always a great draw for fans who enjoy the philosophy of come-uppance, but they promised to take it to each other in the square circle. Hatton, who balloons in weight between bouts (he refers to himself as "Ricky Fatton" and even wears an alter-ego fat suit as a joke), could be seriously undisciplined. To his trainer's great consternation, Hatton, who has many cut scars lining his face, enjoyed downing a Guinness, or six. A British paper once described the Hitman thusly: "Hatton has always been the cheeky chappie of the ring, not so much a Jack-the-lad but a natural comic with the people's touch, one of those homespun heroes who takes his washing home to mum, likes a jar, a jape, and a game of darts down at his local and prefers crispy duck to caviar."

Hatton's friend is Wayne Rooney, the blue-collar soccer star for Manchester United who would occasionally carry Hatton's belts into the ring before a bout. "It costs nothing to be nice to people," Hatton says. "When you start to believe in your own hype it's the worst thing you can do. What's the point of winning world titles and being on the telly if everyone thinks you're a bit of a tosser?" But no one was worried about Hatton and Pacquiao attacking each other. "Ricky's always telling jokes, but in the ring he's cold, merciless and an awful man," said a Hatton intimate. Before their fight, the two fighters attended an event at Hollywood's Roosevelt Hotel. Actors Mickey Rourke and Mark Wahlberg, fans of the fistic arts, graced the evening with their presence. "If there was ever a fight worthy of a red carpet, I would like to think it's this one," said Hatton. "He's the best pound-for-pound fighter in the world. He just beat the biggest name in boxing in Oscar De La Hoya. I'd like to think I'm not too shabby as well. But I think the winner is boxing. I'm sure Manny will do his nation proud; I'm gonna do my nation proud. It's going to be an exceptional fight."

Hatton's trainer, Floyd Mayweather Sr., recited his latest and "greatest" rhyme, ripping Freddie Roach, "Pacquiao's going to go from first class to coach, because of the Roach." Afterward, a loud chant of "Man-ny, Man-ny" rose from the crowd.

"I fight for freedom. I fight for Scotland," Pacquiao said in a deep voice, mimicking Mel Gibson's character in *Braveheart*. The crowd laughed. Good times.

Hatton's usual strategy was pure aggression, but the gentleman from Manchester was trying to also juke-and-jive a little. It was a little uncomfortable, like watching a white guy who had just learned the rudimentary moves of hip-hop. He had lost to Floyd Mayweather Jr.—the bout was stopped after one minute thirty-five seconds of round ten—partly because of a lack of variety in his approach to Mayweather, a very clever boxer. He wanted to make sure that didn't happen again.

"Tactically, I think I know what he will be up to. He throws one/two, shuffles in with his feet, he could cause you problems, but if you get adjusted, fine. I don't see a versatile fighter [in Manny Pacquiao]. Four or five fights ago I was easy to read, but not now. I don't think Manny has fought anyone as fiery, ferocious, rough. Ricky Hatton is a handful for anyone and is all over you . . . there is no doubt in my mind. I've never been more certain, more confident. I'm stronger than him, rarely do I have a height advantage, although it is minute, and I have a huge strength and power advantage." As soon as the fight started, Hatton continued coming forward, bobbing slightly. Pacquiao looked relatively uncomfortable, but Hatton's aggression was also exposing the Hitman's jaw. Pacquiao snuck in a right hook with fifty-five seconds to go in round one. Hatton went down on his knees, as if in prayer. He was seriously dazed. There was a palpable buzz through the crowd that happens in a big fight when someone gets concussed. Pacquiao led with a right and hit him with a straight left near the ropes. *Bam-BAM!* With nine seconds left, Hatton fell again. He steadied himself, sort of, and beat the count. In the corner, Floyd Mayweather Sr., stunned, sprinkled him with water. The Hitman had sixty seconds to regain his senses. He unsteadily rose from his stool. Like a ballet dancer in warm-ups, Hatton shook out his legs.

Roach had watched tape of Hatton and knew he tended to lower his right hand before a punch. He felt confident that Pacquiao would put him away, especially if he followed what they had done in training. "Go out there and feint this guy. Once you feint him, he'll cock his hands, he'll open up, and you'll hit him with the hook." Roach knew that Hatton thought his pupil was predictable. But Pacquiao was too fast. "If Manny goes under a punch, something that Hatton has already committed to, there is nothing you can do about it."

Pacquiao hit Hatton consistently now. With twenty seconds to go in round two, the British fans started singing. The night was festive to say the least. And yet, as the great A. J. Liebling would say, "You are surrounded by people whose ignorance of the ring is exceeded only by their willingness to face facts." Of course, the encouragement did not work. At the ten-second mark of a fight, someone bangs a clapper. It's a warning to the fighters and the audience who can't see a clock. About a half second after the clapper, Pacquiao hit him with a vicious left. It was a cruelly clean, tightly arcing shot that etched itself into the memories of boxing aficionados. Hatton, gone, was down on the canvas. Roach was right, of course. Hatton tended to drop his right hand just before a punch. Pacquiao sensed it, and he had reacted with the fateful blow, which was being compared to Rocky Marciano's flattening of Jersey Joe Walcott in their heavyweight title fight in 1952. Boxing historians believed Pacquiao had the most powerful punch of any smaller fighter in the history of the game.

An unbearable nanosecond of peace, and then Pacquiao was held into the air, but he dismissed his sherpa. With a menacing look that had turned to worry, he gazed over at Hatton and went to the corner and prayed. They worked on Hatton, who appeared comatose. While keeping half an eye on Hatton, Pacquiao hugged Alex Ariza and Bob Arum. The assembled media was already putting Pacquiao into a different class of fighter. Pacquiao was the International Boxing Organization and *Ring* magazine World Light Welterweight champion. It was a world record–tying sixth division title and fourth consecutive win in a different weight class. Roach said, "Manny is a monster. He is the best fighter ever. There is no surprise here." Pacquiao had a body of work, more than a dozen iconic victims, vanquished, artistically, brutally.

Hatton climbed off the floor several minutes later, but the interminable wait was an anxious one for his father, Ray, and mother, Carol, who were seated at ringside alongside his distraught fiancée. When he recovered sufficiently for paramedics to be able to sit him on his stool, he remained unable to communicate coherently. Back in his dressing room before being taken to Valley Hospital he managed to say, "It was a hard loss, but I'm okay. I really didn't see the final punch coming, but it was a great shot. I know I'll be okay."

Pacquiao's next opponent would be Miguel Cotto, the Puerto Rican superstar and the welterweight titleholder, and, if the Filipino won that fight (no guarantee since the PacMan would be going up yet another weight class, for a history-making seventh title in seven different weight divisions), he would, everyone hoped, finally, match up against Floyd Mayweather Jr.—bombastic, narcissistic, American, brilliant.

12

A DANGEROUS PLACE

MANNY PACQUIAO had demolished Oscar De La Hoya in December 2008 and knocked out Ricky Hatton in May 2009. He would take on Puerto Rico's Miguel Cotto for a seventh title, the welterweight, which has a maximum limit of 147 pounds, in November 2009. During the run-up to the Cotto fight, Pacquiao had appeared on the cover of *Time* magazine's Asia edition. When asked to sign it, he preferred writing his name in the interior because he didn't want to ruin the nice cover photograph, and he was still in shock that he was on the cover of the esteemed publication. *Time* called him "the latest savior of boxing, a fighter with enough charisma, intelligence, and backstory to help rescue a sport lost in the labyrinth of pay-per-view. . . . Pacquiao has a myth of origin equal to that of any Greek or Roman hero."

To go from a 106-pounder to 147 pounds—a forty-one pound swing—had finally captured the mainstream media's imagination. The *New York Times*, of late a poor source for boxing stories, produced a headline, "With Pacquiao-Cotto, Boxing Is Ready for a Rebirth, Again." For boxing fans, the paper seemed a little late to the party. During the media tour, the two men visited Puerto Rico. "There was a surprising number of people who went to the press conference just to meet Manny," says José A. Sánchez Fournier, the respected sportswriter for *El Nuevo Día*, who had first met the "always smiling" Pacquiao before his fight with Juan Manuel Marquez several years ago. "Manny was surrounded by a mob of Puerto Rican fans of his, who wanted him to beat Cotto, actually. Of course there was a big pro-Cotto crowd, but Manny had a huge number of fans, as well. There is a perceptible anti-Cotto feeling among sports fans in Puerto Rico. But, even taking that into consideration, the number of pro-Manny fans who showed up to support him in the local press conference sincerely amazed me. And I'm pretty used to dealing with crazed boxing fans."

The Pacquiao-Cotto battle was a first-rate affair. It was full of pomp but mostly circumstance.

On November 14, 2009, at the MGM Grand in Las Vegas, Pacquiao made his ritual entrance. Behind him was Freddie Roach, shaking from his Parkinson's tremors. Pacquiao's father was somewhere in the stands—the first time he had been away from the southern Philippines, the first time to see his son fight. ("Las Vegas is very nice but difficult to find rice," he told me.) Pacquiao looked relaxed and in shape. It was mid-afternoon in the Philippines, and millions upon millions of people—from the rice fields and coconut plantations, from fishing villages to copper mines, to dwarf bars to luxury suites—were glued to the TV. The whole archipelago essentially shut down for the brawl. Many Filipinos, including the vice president, had made the trip to Vegas to bear witness and hopefully get some free airtime as supporters of the National Fist. Said a Filipino sportswriter, "We are having hard times in our country. There is terrorism. There is poverty. There are kidnappings every day. We find solace in Manny Pacquiao."

The judges gave the first round to Cotto. About one minute into the second round, Pacquiao leaned against the ropes and let Miguel Angel Cotto hit him. It went against everything the Filipino had been taught in his storied career, and his cornermen were furious and freaking out. At ringside I could hear the violent *push-push-push* of the gloves smacking Pacquiao's flesh. Buboy blubbered. Cotto was a four-time titleholder. He had beaten Shane Mosley and Zab Judah, two excellent fighters. He wanted to win for his father, who had died eleven months earlier. A few of the blows hit Pacquiao square in the chin. *What in the hell was he doing?* "Just testing his power," Pacquiao would say later.

As it turned out, the punches didn't faze Pacquiao, who barely tipped the scale at 144 pounds. He slipped away from Cotto and started to brutalize the poor man. "He hit harder than we expected, and he was stronger than we expected," said Cotto's trainer, Joe Santiago. He put the Puerto Rican on the canvas twice. For most of the bout, Cotto's face was a bloody, bloated mess, and his white trunks were stained red from his own blood. Pacquiao was so fast that he dove into punching range, delivered a head-snapping blow, and then darted outside again. Angles in, angles out. It was beautiful to behold. "He is in his prime," said Roach.

Pacquiao knocked down Cotto once in the third and again in the fourth. Pacquiao's punches came from different directions: straight lefts, hooks, undercuts, combinations.

MAN-NY! MAN-NY! As the fight wore on, Cotto started backpedaling awkwardly. MAN-NY! MAN-NY! Pacquiao would repeatedly strike Cotto's once handsome face, which was a bloody mess. The Puerto Rican star looked dead-eyed and morose, but he refused to quit. For some reason or other, it made me sad to watch him. "If I was in his corner, I would have thrown in the towel in the ninth round," Roach told me after the fight. "They should have had compassion for him."

In the twelfth round, fifty-five seconds in, the referee called the fight a TKO. Before being rushed to the hospital, Cotto stopped to console his mother, who was weeping in his corner.

Pacquiao's team held him in the air. Pacquiao smiled, winked, and talked about his gratitude to his fans and how he would be singing at a concert that night at the Mandalay Bay. He couldn't stop smiling. At the end of the fight, the crowd at the MGM Grand chanted, "We want Floyd! We want Floyd!" referring to a hoped-for fight with Floyd Mayweather Jr. Pacquiao would return to the Philippines to spend time with his family and start laying the groundwork for his congressional bid. Boxing would wait for his encore.

MANNY PACQUIAO was back in the Sarangani in 2010. It was the first day of his campaign for Congress. Everyone doubted him, which was more than reasonable since he has a sixth-grade education, lost his last election, and had yet to reveal an actual platform. No one believed he would win, but no one wanted to say it because they loved the guy. When asked of his chances, people got a panicked look in their eyes, as if they couldn't bear to hurt his feelings. As befitting their cynical nature, journalists weren't so kind. "Making laws is easy. But it is not what is important," the *Manila Bulletin* quoted him as saying in its entertainment section. They chided the boxing star for rumored womanizing. The message was clear: You're a simpleton boxer, not congressman material. About Pacquiao the *Economist* wrote: "Mr. Pacquiao has tried politics before, and failed. In 2007 he stood to represent his home district in Congress. But neither his popularity nor his money could knock out his opponent, who hailed from an entrenched political clan. Mr. Pacquiao has since devised a political party, the People's Champ Movement, but it seems to have no particular ideas to champion."

Pacquiao had eyes. He realized the economy was getting worse for his people. The world economy was going to hell, and there was a two-year ban on fishing certain types of tuna. Fishing is the economic driver in the southern Philippines. People couldn't find work, and there wasn't as much money coming back from relatives. Most of his people lived below the poverty line.

PACQUIAO WALKED down the street in the small—and depressed—town of Kiamba. Jinkee is from here, and he built a house in town a couple years ago. Pacquiao wore a blue vest with his name stitched in yellow letters on the back. He approached the town plaza. Five thousand eager residents cheered him as he stepped onto an elevated concrete slab. (Ross Greenburg, president of HBO Sports, likens Pacquiao to Ali. "Reminds me of a time I was walking with Muhammad Ali, and he literally stopped traffic," he told me. "People were mesmerized, and it is the same with Manny.") Even at

8 p.m., the heat was sweltering. Kids hung in trees, skinny Filipinos were smoking cigarettes like fiends, moths swirled around flickering lights, chickens were being roasted, and bodyguards laughed with the people. There was much talk about how the incumbents use the people, especially the poor. It was the first day of the 2010 campaign, and this was Pacquiao's third stump speech of the day. In Filipino elections, local bureaucrats drone on and on, sort of like a boxing undercard of small-time fighters. This can go on for hours. Pacquiao was the main event, of course. To keep people interested, Pacquiao tried to liven it up. The world's worst magician performed. Then there was music. As a kid, Pacquiao escaped from his impoverished state through boxing and music. He found solace in the songs of Rod Nepomuceno, so Pacquiao hired the folk singer to entertain the crowd. The people, sweating through their dirty shirts, eyes tearing, sang along. It was a love song.

Then Pacquiao's mother, a natural speaker, made the crowd laugh as she told the crowd about Manny's childhood and what a good boy he has always been. These are all stories that people know by heart now.

It was Manny Pacquiao's turn. At press conferences he can seem distracted, even shy. He makes a quick and funny remark, and people laugh at his broken English and are caught up by his sincerity. But this was something different.

When Pacquiao finally orated, he did so with conviction. He talked about how he knew their plight because he had been poor, too. He was one of them. He *is* one of them. He had a quasi-messianic charisma. The people, thousands of them, soaked in his words.

After the speech, he was interviewed by one of the Filipino networks that always follow him. He strode down the street, parting the mob, to his house. The sweating throngs descended upon his place, pushing through a gap in the fence. Pacquiao had large trays of food so he could feed the hundreds of poor people. He then stayed up until 3 a.m. strategizing with his People's Champ Movement running mates. When the strategy session ended, he took a convoy back to General Santos City. He passed terrorist strongholds known for brazen kidnapping and beheading. The island of Mindanao gives Human Rights Watch researchers plenty of fodder. Its report on the area has the downer of a title "You Can Die Anytime," which features a cover photograph of someone holding up a sign reading "Stop Summary Execution." It's an exceptionally perfect place to be killed by a death squad or get kidnapped by Islamic extremists. On some parts of the island, the level of corruption is so laughably high that when a relative or two is murdered family members won't go to the police. After someone gets shot in the head with a .45, it is not unusual for a relative to receive a rather unfriendly text, such as "The person who receives this message will be the next one to be killed." One of Mindanao cities is called the murder capital of the Philippines—in reality—a notable achievement. Enter Manny Pacquiao who wants to clean up this mess.

The Chiongbian family, his political opponent, had been spending decades pressing pesos into residents' hands at communions, birthdays, marriages, and funerals, and controlling the polling places. Obedience is an important cultural factor. Obeying a strong father figure and loyalty usually trump decades of lousy governmental leadership. Ray Chiongbian, the American-educated man going against Pacquiao, stated, "Although he is popular as a sportsman, it's very different being a politician." He made this condescending statement from his 2,718-acre plantation. The family also has a home in Southern California. "Tiger Woods is the number-one golfer, but he can't be, let's say, a race-car driver. We have our limitations and our skills." The people like Manny. They love Manny. There is nothing he can't seem to do. "He is good at math," a Filipino tells me. "He is a quick learner. You will be surprised. He is underrated as an intelligent person. There is no one who can play the damn piano and strum a guitar from what he hears. Pacquiao! It takes a lifetime to hold a tune on your guitar, and he grabs a guitar and plays immediately. There is a theory that left-handers can harness the other side of the brain. Pacquiao!"

But would they vote for him?

Pacquiao ran for Congress in 2007, but he was not as organized, and the millions he spent on the campaign did not always go into the right hands—his ward leaders did not get paid and were not reliable to protect his voting interests. Political campaigns are notoriously violent (there is always a gun ban, always ignored), and elections are routinely fixed. Sixty families control the entire country, and they are rarely, if ever, unseated, as posts are transferred from family member to family member, generation to inept generation—a good and super-enriching gig, especially if you want to ruin the lives of almost 100 million people. While the central government pours money into the poor southern provinces, the funds often go for private planes, security forces, houses, jewelry, and all sorts of graft. Political families do not want to cede power and will resort to any means necessary to hold on to it. That is why Pacquiao's entrance into this so-called political system worries so many people; he is seen as the embodiment of purity, and he will only blight his image, or get killed. Besides mismanaging his last campaign, people tend not to vote for him because they don't want him to stop boxing. After he lost in 2007, no one had ever seen him so depressed, even after a lost fight. He locked himself in a hotel for a week and wouldn't come out.

Ronnie Nathanielsz, the Filipino boxing commentator and astute political observer, believes Pacquiao has had a grand plan since the beginning, and his real ambitions lie in the political arena, not the athletic one: "The guy had a plan. . . . His boxing career has been subconsciously patterned so he can translate his popularity into votes."

In successive days, Pacquiao criss-crossed his district, which has a population of 411,713, about the size of Rhode Island. He campaigned with Manny Villar, who was running for president. Villar grew up poor and through a construction business became a billionaire. He promised Manny that if he supported him and Villar won the candidacy, he would put Pacquiao in charge of building rural hospitals. The two men also have a fledgling construction business, aimed at building structures for the poor. The country's attention was mostly on the presidential race, of course. The frontrunners were former president Joseph "Erap" Estrada, who had been thrown out of office on the allegations of corruption charges, (including accusations he took kickbacks from gambling lords), Benigno "Noynoy" Aquino III (scion of martyr Benigno and Corazon), and Pacquiao's friend, Villar. With the fate of millions of voters' lives at stake, it was a typical Filipino election: Aquino was accused of being psycho (two psychiatrists' reports—both forgeries—were leaked to the media; the largest television news network disclosed that it came from someone in Villar's camp); and Villar's opponents were hinting that the candidate didn't lead as poor a childhood as he was suggesting (a Villar election song begins, "Have you ever had to swim in a river of garbage?") The election would also be the first with automated vote counters, which meant that election day ballot stuffing would probably decline. It was widely believed that Gloria Arroyo, who Pacquiao had allied himself with for a time, won the presidency in 2005 because of vote rigging. Pacquiao was getting his fair share of attention from the foreign media: *60 Minutes*, ABC News, the *Los Angeles Times*, and *Time* sent correspondents to observe the boxer.

Once, I sat on the outskirts of Manila with some of Pacquiao's old old friends and asked them if Pacquiao had changed through the years. I wondered if the fame had altered him. "Manny Pacquiao gives us money," a man said apologetically. "When I had colon cancer, he sent me money. If you need chemo, he says, 'I will pay for everything.' He is like a Santa. I told him, 'Don't enter politics; you will destroy your name.' He says, 'I will be a different politician. That is my dream.'"

THERE WAS A CALL from the Philippines.

Pacquiao is involved with *something*.

"An incident" had gone down in Sarangani province that involved Tata Yap, his close friend and my fellow horse-fighting aficionado. Yap and Pacquiao have the same comet tattoo inked on their left arm. "When we drink beer, we drink from the same glass," Yap says. The impoverished area in which Pacquiao lived the first ten years of his life are, to some extent, under the control of the Yap family. But Yap has been in a political power struggle with his brother, Mayor Enrique Yap Jr., who he hasn't talked with for several years. They dislike each other immensely. Not much happens in their area without their knowledge, control, and backstabbing schemes.

At 10:58 p.m. on a Sunday evening, a week before the 2010 Filipino election, six armed men in three vehicles blocked Enrique Yap's vehicle, according to veteran General Santos journalist Edwin Espejo. They were held at gunpoint, but Yap was able to call for police assistance, which rushed to his aid, and the six suspects were arrested. The police said that one of the two vehicles recovered by authorities was registered under the name of Pacquiao's wife, Jinkee. Several campaign stickers of Pacquiao, as well as one armalite rifle and one .45 caliber pistol, were also recovered from the two Toyota vans. The heat came on Pacquiao immediately. Pacquiao denied any involvement in the ambush, and Espejo says the alledged ambush involving Enrique Yap as the reported target has never been proven.

Then there was an explosion that nearly hit the convoy of Sarangani governor Miguel Rene Dominguez. People started whispering that Pacquiao had done it. Pacquiao claimed it was all a set-up and accused his opponents of "ambushing" him. "What they did was 'ambush me' since the motorcycle used in the explosion was owned by their supporters," he says. "They wanted to frame me up." The police have not pointed to any suspect.

Pacquiao says the vans were under his wife's name because she has a rent-a-car business.

"I have God wherever I am," says Pacquiao. "They should not resort to creating stories."

As the May 10 election drew closer that spring of 2010, there was word that Pacquiao was edging up in the polls. The suspects who allegedly had ambushed his political rival were about ready to be charged with possessing firearms during an election, but interestingly enough Pacquiao's legal counsel intervened and requested that the case be dismissed in one of the more amazing utterances in the annals of legal mumbo-jumbo: "Nothing in the affidavit of arrest alleged that the arresting officers saw the respondents carrying firearms," said Pacquiao's attorney. "Then they searched, first, before arresting. It should be arresting, first, before searching to make it a warrantless arrest." Why Pacquiao's attorney would step into the case raised more suspicion that Pacquiao was involved with the supposed ambush and wanted it to go away.

This was the sort of thing that people feared: The purity of Manny Pacquiao would be usurped by politics.

PACQUIAO SPENT forty-four days campaigning and spending millions, probably more than $7 million of his own money, rarely sleeping and eating a lot of fried food instead of his favorite, and more healthy, *tuna kinilaw*. At the end of the election, he would be hospitalized with an ulcer. He directed his campaign from his mansion, off the NLSA Road, where the smell of trash mixed with the nearby fish market that sells tilapia and tuna. (His mother has her place nearby, too, next to the PacMan convenience store and collection of hovels where they sell wood for cooking. A rooster or two strut through the dank water.) The PacMan also had a cramped two-room office, dubbed, "The Pentagon," which was plagued by power shortages. At the beginning of the election, poll numbers stated that Pacquiao would lose by a 30 percent to 70 percent margin. Bob Arum, politically liberal, offered moral support. Arum has a soft spot for athletes involved in social causes. In every press conference before the election, Arum kept saying, ad nauseum, that he would soon be calling Pacquiao "the Honorable," or "Congressman Pacquiao." Arum also went to General Santos to support Pacquiao. He called it "one of the most exciting trips of my life. Now I am considering if I should pack it in as boxing promoter and become a political adviser. Ali was a wonderful person, but it was more about Ali. This kid spent a fortune running for office. And he did it not to aggrandize himself but because he really believes he can make a difference."

To people who worried that if Pacquiao won he would give up boxing, Arum said that he talked with Pacquiao about the sport, and Pacquiao emphasized that he wanted to take on Mayweather.

On election night, May 10, 2010, Pacquiao won by a landslide. He grinned, "A Congressman!"

13

FIGHTER OF THE DECADE

PACQUIAO HAD BEEN suffering from an ulcer and had spent a few days in a Metro Manila hospital. The Fifteenth Philippine Congress would start on June 30, 2010, and he would need to take a rudimentary government class so he could figure out exactly how to do his job. Weirdly enough, many political analysts believed Pacquiao would be the president of the Philippines in ten years' time, when he was eligible for the country's highest office. The future race might be between Pacquiao and Ferdinand Marcos's son, "Bongbong." After recovering from his ailment, Pacquiao took his family on vacation to New York before the congressional session began.

He went to New York to attend the Boxing Writers Association of America Awards Dinner, considered the Academy Awards of boxing, held on a Friday in June.

On Thursday, Pacquiao had gone to a New York Friar's Club Tribute/Roast of Bob Arum. There was a dinner before the event. Pacquiao avoided the meal (the Filipino workers at the club were dying to see him, and they were ten deep outside wanting to catch a glimpse of the PacMan). As usual,

Pacquiao arrived late. A few people in his entourage and adviser Michael Koncz, who sported a bad shiner, accompanied him.

Pacquiao hadn't really known what to expect at the roast, but he had a great time and stayed late.

The next night, Pacquiao would receive the award for the boxer of the decade.

The event took me back several years ago, when I was at the Wild Card one late afternoon chatting with Freddie Roach. A heavy rain had drenched Los Angeles. We were talking about an upcoming bout, but he really wanted to talk about Manny Pacquiao who wasn't an international star yet. Back then, Roach was still more shy and suspicious than outgoing around writers. This was before Pacquiao graced the cover of *Time* magazine, before Kobe, Shaq, and Denzel were seeking his friendship, before he won seven belts in seven different weight divisions, before much of the world was calling him the greatest boxer to ever step inside the ring. I named some other fighters—some of them household names, many of whom Roach had trained and knew intimately—but Freddie emitted an exasperated sigh. The blighted areas of America were still producing some boxing talent, but to find the real up-and-comers, one's worldview had to shift to the Third World. (And post-NAFTA, even Mexico was going a little soft.) An old boxing writer once said boxing "serves a place in our life, helping to stave off the effeminacy that is one of the dangers of nations that grow old and soft and unwilling to endure hardships." I didn't quite agree with that assessment of the sweet science. It wasn't like Mexico, the Philippines, and Puerto Rico were killing us in world trade or that life was that soft for the majority of people. But I did have it all wrong: No one knew it yet, but Pacquiao was the man to watch, a once-in-an-era fighter. Roach's hand shook a little. His eyes sparkled when he talked about him.

Pacquiao was already a great fighter—but the greatest?—he was scary quick and possessed a concussive left hook, but his defensive skills were suspect, and his right hand was still considered an afterthought. But Roach and Pacquiao were working on a grand plan, which had started on that night in 2005, as the trainer sat forlornly in a Las Vegas hospital. Pacquiao was getting both of his bruised eyes stitched up. Pacquiao had just lost to Erik Morales in the year's best and bloodiest fight. Pacquiao and Roach rededicated themselves that evening. Roach saw that Pacquiao wanted to achieve something everlasting. The men set out to create the perfect boxer—a guy who fought with passion and certitude. Roach would figure out ways to fix his fighter's flaws and bring logic to his punches. Freddie Roach and Manny Pacquiao's creation has gone down in boxing lore as something of a pugilistic Picasso.

From that day on, I started following Pacquiao in earnest. Besides studying his fights, I kept up with him by reading Filipino newspapers. But outside of white America, boxing's stars are cultural icons—there exists a secret language, a sweet science subculture. Manny Pacquiao had made boxing relevant again, if that mattered. A possible fight with the American Floyd Mayweather Jr. was getting people so jazzed that the sport was being talked about in barrooms and even in the *New York Times*. Older television executives were comparing Pacquiao's star quality and crowd-pleasing style

to the era of Hagler-Hearns-Duran-Leonard. It was estimated that each fighter would earn $40 to $50 million, the
biggest payday in boxing history. West Coast baseball teams
were inviting Pacquiao to throw out the first pitch (the San
Francisco Giants' star pitcher Tim Lincecum, a Filipino
American, raved about the action on Pacquiao's ball; Manny
had loved baseball as a kid), and American politicians, such
as Senator Dianne Feinstein, honored him with commenda-
tions so they could endear themselves to millions of Filipino
Americans. Pacquiao had his naked torso featured in *ESPN:
The Magazine* in an issue that explored the engineering of
several athletic physiques. While he didn't fight in the 2008
Summer Olympics, Pacquiao was the flag-bearer for the
Philippines' national team at the opening ceremonies in
Beijing—the first Filipino non-Olympian to do so.

In the course of Manny Pacquiao's rise, he became something even bigger than a sports page myth: The hero worship
he received in his homeland has actually been compared to
the disenfranchised's love for Nelson Mandela. His image is
on Philippine currency. Islamic militants call a truce with the
government during his fights. He crossed so many boundaries
that he defied stereotype. With the exception of Pelé, no
sports star from the Third World had ever achieved such
fame. "We live in a culture in which people are looking for
something wrong, but Pacquiao is a wonderful kid," says Bert
Sugar. "He approaches you. He smiles, he is humble. He is a
cute little guy—I want to pinch his cheek. Pacquiao will say hi
to reporters, you don't have to go through a phalanx of bodyguards. There is no façade there. Everyone is fond of him.
America has embraced him. He transcends being a Filipino."

Pacquiao (51–3–2) is not undefeated, but his record over the last ten years is outstanding.

He had lost to Medgoen Singsurat in his twenty-eighth pro fight, but he had fought twenty-eight since then and lost only one fight, to the formidable Erik Morales. For the Morales loss, all three judges' scorecards read 115–113. So one single round was all that separated Pacquiao from an unbeaten ring record over the past eleven years. His last eleven victories were either over reigning or former world champions, and just three of them—Juan Manuel Marquez, Oscar Larios, and Erik Morales—went the distance. It wasn't the impressive record as much as the high-octane style. "He's like a grand painting," says Bob Arum.

ON A MUGGY NIGHT in early June, the 85th Annual Boxing Writers Association of America's annual banquet was underway at the futzy Roosevelt Hotel on East 45th Street. Manny Pacquiao, the man of the evening, was supposed to be awarded the fighter of the year and the fighter of the decade. He was nowhere to be found. Bob Arum, lonesome, sat at the Pacquiao table, at the front of the room.

Halfway through the evening Pacquiao, accompanied by his wife and kids and three gigantic bodyguards, appeared. Everyone rushed him as he arrived. They tried to take photographs or get an autograph. Filipino newsmen sitting in the balcony were furiously taking photographs and jotting down notes. Pacquiao smiled.

Smokin' Joe Frazier presented the "Sugar Ray Robinson Fighter of the Year" award to the Filipino. It was Pacquiao's third BWAA fighter of the year award, tying him with

Muhammad Ali and Evander Holyfield for the most in the history of the organization.

He didn't give a speech, but he held his award, and once again people rushed him, his guards pushing people away. His children, sitting at another table, seemed sleepy. With a great deal of humility, he introduced himself to Tommy Hearns and Ray Mancini. They had never met. He told them he was a big fan. They came away impressed.

Then Roach was given the trainer of the year award. It was his record-setting fourth "Eddie Futch Trainer of the Year" award. He was dressed in a suit and tie. He thanked his mother who beamed. Roach recounted his life story: about his dad being an amateur boxer, about learning from the award's namesake Eddie Futch, about training Virgil Hill (his first student and champion), about opening up the Wild Card—"Hoping that young prospects would come through my door, and this guy named Manny Pacquiao shows up one day. After one round with the mitts, I knew he was special." He looked down at Pacquiao, his hand shaking, "Manny you're the greatest thing that ever happened to me in my life."

Eventually Pacquiao strode onto the stage. He was no longer a boy. He had transformed somehow over the last six months into a more serious man. The smile, the one that had endeared him to his people since he was a boy, still appeared on his face. It always disarmed an audience. He came from the City of Dust. Now he was in New York City. Pacquiao, a one-in-ninety million kind of guy, stood before the crowd.

"Poverty confronted my family," he said. "Poverty challenged my youth."

He talked about his struggles and his trust in God (He formed him from "nothing to something") and dreaming big. He thanked his wife, four children, Bob Arum, and Freddie Roach. His jetlagged children's heads were down. They had fallen asleep. He told the audience that the world was a family and strength comes with how it is used. His boxing career, he suggested, fulfilled a greater purpose. Outside the hotel, Filipinos were gathering. "Hello sir*rrrr*. Is Pacquiao coming? Is Jinkee with him?" Cameras ready, they seemed incredulous that they might actually see Manny Pacquiao. There were some hotel workers who were peeking into the banquet room to listen. Seemingly on cue, Pacquiao talked about his countrymen all over the world and how their sacrifices had inspired him. "I am Emmanuel Dapidran Pacquiao; I am proud to be a Filipino."

EPILOGUE:
THE MAYWEATHER QUESTION

IN THE WILD CARD BOXING CLUB, over by the speed bags, there is a small photo of Floyd Mayweather Jr. His smiling face looks down at the gym. It is a source of inspiration to Manny Pacquiao, who is also known to put pictures of his upcoming opponents in his bedroom. Mayweather has been Pacquiao's greatest detractor outside of the ring and someone who seems reluctant to face the Filipino in it. In the first decade of the twenty-first century, there was a fierce debate among boxing aficionados about who held the mythic prize of best pound-for-pound boxer, and most analysts came down on the side of Pacquiao or Mayweather. Pacquiao was known for his charisma, offensive flourishes, and prodigious workouts. Mayweather was known for his charisma, brilliant defense, and prodigious workouts. For the boxing lifers, no one since Sugar Ray Robinson had worked as hard outside of the ring as Pacquiao and Mayweather. The sports public now wanted to see the two men meet in the ring. It would be an epic battle between offense and defense, a personality clash between a brash American and a classy Filipino.

After Pacquiao beat Miguel Cotto on November 14, 2009, the Filipino came to the pressroom wearing a grey triloby hat. He was smiling despite the bandage over his ear.

He never looked so happy. The American boxing writers were feeding off the excitement. They were covering a real sport again. Talk turned immediately to a Pacquiao fight against Mayweather.

"The two best pound-for-pound fighters in the world in the same weight class in the prime of their careers," HBO's Ross Greenburg said about a potential Pacquiao-Mayweather bout. "It just doesn't get any better than that."

"The way I look at it now, boxing is really on a roll," Bob Arum said. "We would be idiots now to slow the momentum, and the only way we can keep the momentum is to make this fight."

In late 2009, the talk of the fight world became a proposed March 2010 welterweight title clash between Pacquiao and Mayweather Jr. Superlatives were thrown around, including the likelihood of it being the most lucrative boxing match ever. But it started to become the greatest fight that never was.

Bob Arum and Oscar De La Hoya's Golden Boy team started negotiating. There was a lot of rancor between the promoters. The men, who essentially control boxing, still have an on-again, off-again relationship. But both of them realized that matching Pacquiao (in Arum's stable) and Mayweather (a Golden Boy fighter) would be enormously lucrative, to the tune of $40 million per fight. Arum wanted to hold the bout in the Dallas Cowboys' new stadium. Arum said he wanted to bring boxing back to regular sports fans. He believed a stadium fight would be a good showcase for the sport. Arum and the Golden Boy's Richard Schaefer were supposed to board a private plane to meet with Cowboys owner Jerry Jones. Only Arum showed up at the airport and he was incensed. Then Mayweather dropped the bombshell of bombshells: as a precondition to fighting the Filipino he wanted Olympic-style random blood testing. The request itself implied that Pacquiao was juicing. Pacquiao was upset. He said he abided by boxing commission laws, not rules introduced by a rival. Caught off guard, Pacquiao said his honor and name had been tarnished. In Asia, losing face is no joke.

In the Wild Card, during the first negotiating debacle, there was a great deal of anger.

The Wild Card subspecies tend to take after Freddie Roach, who believes public trash-talking is an expression of cowardice. Mayweather had left Pacquiao to answer questions about performance-enhancing drugs (in his jilted English, he was no match for the jocular Mayweather) and left American sports fans perpetually confused. The fight could have become the seminal event in modern boxing. But the self-destructive nature of the fight game had brought pessimism to the Wild Card. Everyone in the place loves and makes a living from Manny Pacquiao, and they wanted him to be a part of history. So everyone in the Wild Card gym showed a higher level of pissed-off-ness than usual during the late days of 2009. Amid the bag-punching, jump-roping, hand wrapping, and spitting, negative comments about Mayweather were flying like beads of sweat.

Unless pressed, the Filipinos in attendance didn't really want to talk about it. The cursing came from people with pallid skin, most blemished with tattoos, in the form of Boston accents—"Bast'd!" "Aaashole."

Freddie Roach has been around long enough to see through the Mayweather gamesmanship: "It's just that Mayweather is trying to make a bigger fight, and he is trying to sell all of his bullshit." Roach spent time psychoanalyzing his own fighter. "If Manny gives blood, for three days—*he is a fucking hypochondriac*—he will feel weak, and he will be mopey; he won't smile—he'll be angry. He will be pissed off for three days. It's just the way it is. I don't know if it is mental or physical. For me, giving blood doesn't bother me; some people pass out when they give blood—for him, I lose him for three days. I lose him to sparring."

When trainers talk about their charges they often use the first person, as if they are joined together. "If I give blood on day thirteen then I lose him for day thirteen, twelve, and eleven, and those are crucial days coming up to a fight. I can't really afford to let him do that, and I would never let him get into the ring not mentally 100 percent ready. Every fighter who's dominated their divisions in boxing, like Sugar Ray Leonard, Tommy Hearns, have always challenged people at the higher weights for the world title. I mean Leonard, six titles, six weight divisions; Hearns six titles, six weight divisions; Roberto Duran, five; Oscar De La Hoya, five; Floyd Mayweather, five. It's natural. People get bigger, people get thicker."

Between grunts, everyone was sort of straining to hear Freddie's thoughts.

Roach was genuinely mad because he didn't like having Pacquiao's reputation and his own sullied. Roach had to endure abuse from the Mayweathers at many a press conference in which they taunted him by calling him "punch

drunk," "a joke coach," and "the roach." "We will abide by
the [boxing] commission rules on a blood test after the fight
and urine tests anytime," Roach told me at the time. A statement from Pacquiao's promoters specified that the Filipino
fighter had already agreed to take blood tests as prescribed,
including one in January when the fight was to have been
officially announced; and one no later than February 13,
which was thirty days before the proposed match. The additional blood test request, Roach claimed, was simply an
excuse to scuttle the fight. "We're gonna knock this bum out,
he knows it, and he is scared."

Alex Ariza was asked for a summation: "I think Mayweather is afraid. Here is how I see it. If you look at
Leonard and Hearns, well, Hearns and Leonard are still
talking about that one fight their whole lives. Mayweather
would be associated with the biggest fight of our era, and
he's going to be *the loser* of that fight. I have *no* doubt. I
wish we were fighting Mayweather today. I have never seen
Manny so fast and in such good shape. When it comes to
fighting, Manny doesn't give two shits. He doesn't care.
Doesn't matter how much money he has, his acting, his
singing. . . . Fighting? Fighting! That's like playing with a
lion. He doesn't know how to go soft speed. It's all or nothing. Mayweather on the other hand will have to hear, 'You
lost to Pacquiao, you got knocked out by Pacquiao.' *The
rest of his life.*"

Floyd Mayweather Jr. professed grave disappointment in
Pacquiao's reluctance: "I understand Pacquiao not liking to
have his blood taken, because frankly I don't know anyone
who really does," said Mayweather. "But in a fight of this

magnitude, I think it is our responsibility to subject ourselves to sportsmanship at the highest level. I have already agreed to the testing, and it is a shame that he is not willing to do the same. It leaves me with great doubt as to the level of fairness I would be facing in the ring that night."

Pacquiao's camp expressed long faces and hurt feelings about the accusations. The accusations and counteraccusations played out in the press, implying that the cultural icon of the Philippines was cheating. "I am taking a stand," Mayweather said, adding, "I should get to choose who I want to fight." They went to an arbitrator in Santa Monica, California, but nothing could get worked out. By allowing the negotiations to collapse, Pacquiao and Mayweather quickly became defined as the boxers who wouldn't fight each other. Boxing had been poised for something substantial, but it became a big joke. "I think Floyd is scared of Manny," says Roach. "I think the public is disgusted by the controversy, but they still want the fight to happen."

In the Wild Card, the entourage strutted around wearing T-shirts that said "100% GOD, NO STEROIDS."

"He is accusing me of using drugs or whatever and trying to ruin my name in boxing," Pacquiao told me one day in the claustrophobic locker room. Everyone wanted the fight, but wasn't Mayweather just making it bigger? Ali once said: "When you chase that beautiful lady, you put the cologne on your face, and for a little while nothing else matters. Then it is over, one way or the other, and you wonder why you got so excited. It's the same when two guys get into the ring; whatever else is happening in the world, you want to know the answer to just one question: who's gonna win, who's gonna win? Fighting will always have that because, you know, it is just so basic."

Mayweather, a kaleidoscope of emotions, relishes in getting under his opponent's skin. What Mayweather had done was inject an accusatory undertone of doping that was bound to irritate the Pacquiao camp, because it tarnished the seven-time champion's dramatic victories. "Mayweather is using this to harass Manny," said an apoplectic Arum. "This fight is down the drain. It makes no sense at all. My kid is clean as a whistle."

Mayweather is one of the smartest boxers around. "He is brilliant at draining the drama from a fight, but he also wins," says Larry Merchant, the HBO boxing analyst. By making a request that he expected Pacquiao to turn down, he may have proven that he is just as good a tactician outside the ring as in it.

"I'm disappointed of what he is accusing me," says Pacquiao. "I feel bad. I know that's his style. We cannot change that . . . we are different. Maybe he's afraid of me? Maybe he's not ready. I don't need to fight Mayweather."

Or did he?

WHEN THEY TRAINED for their subsequent fights, they constantly fielded questions about each other. It haunted them. Every decade, sometimes every two or three, a pair of fighters at the height of their powers and popularity come together and slug it out in battles described like the hymns of ancient lore: Louis-Schmeling, Ali-Frazier, Leonard-Hearns. . . . Pacquiao-Mayweather were thus anointed. But in a boxing world run amok, they hadn't been able to put together the fight. In the aftermath of their failed negotiations, both camps and their promotional machines would do anything to tear down the other fighter. Pacquiao had even brought in a hotshot attorney, who had worked on the O. J. Simpson defense, to sue Mayweather for slander. "I'm not angry at Floyd," Pacquiao said unconvincingly to those who know him.

Mayweather has never lost a professional bout, and avoiding punches might not be "fan friendly," but it is a better path to avoid boxing dementia. He might not be loved by all, but he has done well managing his controversial image. He is a braggart. He owns a seventeen-thousand-square-foot house, owns more than a million dollars worth of wristwatches, carries around $30,000 in his pockets, he gambles like a fiend, and he hangs out with the rapper 50 Cent.

In all truth, Pacquiao and Mayweather have more in common than anyone would know.

They both come from troubled backgrounds, have large entourages, they had early success in the ring, and have notable soft sides (Mayweather is known to cry openly, is involved in helping the homeless, has helped down-on-their-luck boxers, and as a kid was always bringing home stray dogs and cats). And they are both on the lookout for a father figure. Mayweather's father, Floyd Mayweather Sr., spent a five-and-a-half-year sentence in a federal penitentiary on a drug-dealing conviction. He was once a contender himself, but he was stopped in a 1978 fight against Sugar Ray Leonard after breaking his hand in the eighth round. He fought on until the tenth round. Four months after the defeat, he was shot in the leg in a family dispute. He was holding Little Floyd at the time. About his son, he has said, "He was training to be a fighter in the crib. No kidding. He was throwing jabs even then. And then when he got a little older, he'd be beating the doorknobs." Big Floyd trained his son as a child in their hometown of Grand Rapids, Michigan. "I was on my own at age sixteen," Mayweather Jr. once told the *New York Times*. As an amateur, at age sixteen, Floyd Jr. won the National Golden Gloves in 1993 and won it again in 1994 and 1996. He earned a bronze medal in the Atlanta Olympics. After his father was incarcerated, Roger Mayweather, Floyd Jr.'s uncle, took over the training duties.

Adding layers to the eternal soap opera, Bob Arum managed Mayweather Jr. during the early part of his career, but Little Floyd didn't like the way Arum hemmed him in. Early in his career, Mayweather found himself in a private jet with two Arum clients—Sugar Ray Leonard and De La Hoya. They saw his promise and gave him suggestions on how to dress and handle the media, Mayweather told ESPN. "You can be the next Sugar Ray Leonard," De La Hoya told him. "Keep winning and keep smiling." Recalling the conversation, De La Hoya said, "I was talking, but I knew it was pointless. It was going in one ear and out the other." Mayweather is a charismatic character who is full of need. His best punches come from his mouth (he hasn't had a pure knockout since 1999). Mayweather calls himself Money and proves his self-worth by shaking wads of "Benjamins" into people's faces. He always pleads when he talks. Journalists approach him, and his neural pathways start firing. He seems to be desperate to be liked but he continually says unlikable things.

After compiling a 39–0 record (25 KOs), he retired in 2008. He had been branching out of boxing with an appearance on the reality series *Dancing with the Stars*, followed by a heavily publicized wrestling match against "Big Show" at World Wrestling Entertainment's WrestleMania 24. But while Mayweather was on hiatus and spending time dancing and pretend wrestling, Pacquiao's reputation grew with every fight—crowds loved the PacMan's style, whose insane risk-reward ratio creates drama. (Says Roach, "You talk to boxing fans, and they can't stand Mayweather. They would rather watch paint dry. That's how boring it is.") The Pac-Man was getting attention on all fronts: the American people, fellow professional athletes who liked Pacquiao's humility and exciting style, and the boxing writers who named the Filipino the best active pound-for-pound fighter.

Mayweather emits a crestfallen sigh: "I got respect for Sugar Ray Robinson. I've got respect for Muhammad Ali. But I'm a man just like they're men. I put on my pants just like they put on their pants. What makes them any better than I am? Because they fought a thousand fights? In my era, it's totally different. It's pay-per-view now, so things change. It's out with the old and in with the new. Things change. Like I said, Muhammad Ali is one hell of a fighter. But Floyd Mayweather is the best. Sugar Ray Robinson is one hell of a fighter, but Floyd Mayweather is the best."

After going on hiatus, Mayweather decided to make a comeback. He brought his father back into camp to plot strategy in his fight against Juan Manuel Marquez in 2009. (Mayweather won in a unanimous decision.) He expected the adulation to return, and it did to an extent, but Pacquiao had also gained a significant fanbase, and the Boxing Writers Association named Pacquiao the best fighter of the decade, a designation that Mayweather could hardly stomach. "Manny Pacquiao struggled twice against Juan Manuel Marquez, he got knocked out twice, he got outboxed by Erik Morales, but then they still give him Boxer of the Decade. I don't understand . . ."

After the proposed megafight fell apart, Pacquiao fought Joshua Clottey, and Mayweather took on "Sugar" Shane Mosley.

PACQUIAO FOUGHT FIRST against Clottey on March 13, 2010, at Dallas's Cowboys Stadium. The world didn't know what to think. Clottey, who is from Ghana, didn't have much name recognition. A part-time locksmith trained him. Because the world wanted to see Pacquiao versus Mayweather, the fight was a serious letdown. (At the Texas hotel where Pacquiao stayed, Bob Arum walked around muttering, "Fuck Golden Boy," like it was his mantra.)

On the day of the fight, a Filipino friend told me to meet him at Mass. Pacquiao had rented a large hall in his hotel for his prefight ritual. Someone pleaded to the people not to take photographs so as not to damage Pacquiao's eyes. That request was roundly ignored. Pacquiao walked to take communion with Roach, Ariza, Buboy. The morning Mass was the medieval Spanish Catholic kind that borders on mystic, the kind that blesses a boxer's gold groin protector in front of five hundred Filipinos like it were a newborn. On the evening of the fight, Pacquiao ended up not having needed much blessed protection from anything, a puffy eye the only residue from a pummeling—and I think 1,231 punches, including one thirty-six-hit combination I counted from ringside, counts as a pummeling—of Clottey to retain the welterweight championship of the world.

He was the greatest and unlikeliest pound-for-pound fighter in the world, standing in the middle of Cowboys Stadium on the receiving end of some Texas-style pageantry, loving every second of it. It was the same boyish smile that people had grown to enjoy through the years. People like Pacquiao because of his sincerity but mostly because he likes to have a good time. And good times are what make him so good. Good times are especially important right before a big fight. Like the two months preceding the fight—a lot of which I spent by his side, too—when his practice boxers pretended to be Clottey. I asked Roach, the head trainer, how hard Pacquiao really works in sparring sessions. "Maybe sixty percent," he said. "He can fuckin' hit."

On that Saturday night he was pretty relaxed. Roach told me he'd never seen a boxer this happy this close to a title bout. I couldn't help but believe him: Here was a young man who used to sell doughnuts on Manila street corners, making bad jokes for his buddies as he wrapped his own hands in tape so tight they were practically purple—while the Dallas Cowboys cheerleaders were checking him out. (They also sang the national anthem.) "But when he enters the ring and crosses himself," Roach reminded me, "it's all business." And it was. From ringside, you could barely even follow Pacquiao's red gloves, made from leather and woven horsehair, they were moving so fast. Clottey actually chose a particular type of padded glove just to help defend his face—not that he went down, but not that he stood much of a chance in the decision, either. "He is fast. He is fast," Clottey said after the fight. "He is strong, too." Pacquiao won an easy decision. It was hardly a spellbinder.

Pacquiao, for his part, already had his sunglasses back on as his guys sped him off to evening Mass. There was no time to waste, after all: His band had a big show on Saturday night, too. Pacquiao told me his first song would be "La Bamba," and that the concert would go well into the Texas night.

FLOYD MAYWEATHER was up next.

Mayweather had asked his opponent Shane Mosley, who was involved but he said unwittingly in the BALCO scandal, to take random blood tests. Mosley agreed. Mayweather used the fight as a way to win back the public. Bringing up the name Manny Pacquiao was essentially verboten. (At the Los Angeles kick-off press conference, legitimate Filipino journalists were banned from talking with him.) As expected, he won the Mosley fight, but when he made his ring entrance—complete with men throwing fake one hundred dollar bills into the crowd—he was roundly booed.

In the MGM Grand, full to the rafters, Mayweather Jr. (40–0; 25 KOs) jauntily strode toward the middle of the ring that night on May 1, 2010. The boxer wore red faux leather trunks trimmed in black fur, his five foot eight body rippled with muscles and a confident grin. His weight was announced at 146. In the opposite corner stood Mosley (46–5; 39 KOs), about the same size, give or take a pound at fight time, but five years his senior.

Mayweather is arguably the greatest defensive technician in the history of the sport, but many boxing fans don't always appreciate his gift for dodging punches—and worthy opponents. Enter Mosley, Mayweather's quickest and most formidable foe to date. "I believe I am faster," Mosley, a natural welterweight, told me before the fight. "I have never faced him, so I don't know. But I am fast." Most of my colleagues in press row, Nevada bookmakers, and the betting public didn't think Mosley, thirty-eight, was fast and powerful enough anymore and made the veteran a 4–1 underdog. And by the beginning of round three, Mosley was breathing through his mouth, a sure sign of fatigue.

After the opening bell, Mosley, clad in black shorts trimmed in baby blue, stepped forward to pursue the younger man. Mosley connected with some right hands in the early rounds, but mostly he punched the air. In the second round, Mosley nearly pulled off the upset. The crowd chanted, "Mo-sley! Mo-sley!" after he landed a big right, which seriously stunned Mayweather. "It's a contact sport," says Mayweather. "You're going to get hit, but when you get hit, you suck it up and keep fighting." To regain his composure, he told me after the fight, he thought about his children, and it calmed him down. The blow was the lone highlight of the night for Mosley. His age (he complained of a tight neck) and Mayweather's right hand over Mosley's jab caught up with him as the fight wore on. "He was too quick, and I was too tight," Mosley admitted later.

Mayweather, who is usually speeding around the ring like a Nevada jackrabbit, decided to stay in the center of the canvas and go toe-to-toe. It seemed to shock everyone, including his opponent. Mayweather cleverly jabbed and counterpunched Mosley, and though the fight went twelve rounds, Mayweather, who won in a unanimous decision, dominated it.

Mosley was a marquee name and a top-ten pound-for-pound fighter, but he was viewed as over the hill. The hope was that if Pacquiao and Mayweather both won their respective fights, they would work out their differences and fight in the fall. "My nails are going to be bitten down to the bone, waiting until May 2," Ross Greenburg, president of HBO Sports, which hoped to televise the Pacquiao-Mayweather spectacle, told me.

BECAUSE MAYWEATHER had battled a more worthy opponent, some considered him the best pound-for-pound fighter in the world. The stage was set for the two men to finally fight. Pacquiao told Bob Arum to make it happen. He would take the blood test. Pacquiao, a fervent card player, was desperate to fight Mayweather, and he decided to call what he thought was Mayweather's bluff.

"They have to deliver," HBO's Greenburg said. "The American public wants that fight."

But the relationship between both camps remained frosty.

About Pacquiao, Roger Mayweather said, "I don't know how good he is. I can't say how good he is because every time I see him fighting he must have something in his system. Anytime a guy doesn't want to take a test, that tells you already about the guy."

After the Mayweather-Mosley fight, Mayweather—clad in a suit, tie, and fuchsia shirt with diamond-encrusted "MM" cufflinks—talked about his reputation (he was upset that so many Americans like Pacquiao) and his impending vacation (perhaps a Disney cruise with his family).

"If Manny Pacquiao takes the blood and urine tests, we can fight," said Mayweather. "If Manny wants to fight, it's not that hard to find me."

Freddie Roach who understands, but doesn't always like the hyperbole around boxing, had become philosophic about Mayweather's claims. "People say, 'How can a guy go from 106 all the way to 147 without being on steroids?' But if you take that thinking into consideration, at age sixteen, Floyd Mayweather fought in the amateurs at 106, and then he went to 154 [to fight Oscar De La Hoya,] so he must be on steroids, too, I guess? But I'm not going to say that, because he's just a good fighter, and I respect that. The thing is, it's not unusual for the best fighters of their era to dominate many different weight divisions because that's where all of the challenges are. I think that Mayweather was just trying to make the fight bigger. I think that he's trying to make the Pacquiao fight bigger down the line. I think that he's just doing his thing. *I have trouble giving Manny Pacquiao vitamins.* The Mayweathers are just trying to tarnish his reputation. It's the first time that I've really seen him angry with a fighter. He says, 'If we fight, I will knock Floyd out.'"

DESPITE THE ANIMOSITY, and maybe because of it, there was optimism that their differences could be worked out on paper. Negotiations seemed to start again for a bout in November 2010, but then it all turned even more bizarre.

Fans were demanding the fight. The rapper Snoop Dogg made a video pleading with the men to rumble in the ring.

Michael Wilbon, a host on an ESPN commentary show, said Mayweather would be a "coward" if he didn't face Pacquiao.

Earlier in the year HBO's Greenburg had asked Arum how serious Pacquiao was about fighting Mayweather. The Filipino wanted the fight. Because the rancor from the previous negotiations was still raw, Greenburg told Arum he would act as an intermediary. Arum negotiated the fight, via Greenburg, through Mayweather adviser Al Haymon. Arum wouldn't reveal the exact terms, but he says the blood-testing issue was settled. The two parties seemed to come to a gentleman's agreement, but nothing was signed and it was unclear if Mayweather Jr. was onboard. Oscar De La Hoya went on a Univision television show and in Spanish said, "Up until now, it's been a very difficult negotiation process for various reasons but right now we're very close." Given Pacquiao's tight schedule because of his congressional duties and in a ploy to put pressure on the American fighter, Arum gave Mayweather an arbitrary two-week deadline to approve and sign the contract or he would start negotiating with other fighters. The deadline was midnight on Friday, July 16.

How could the fight not happen? It's never a fair fight when boxing people and logic go toe-to-toe: Logic inevitably gets knocked to the canvas. Shortly after Friday passed into Saturday in Las Vegas, a weary Arum relayed the depressing news to a handful of bleary-eyed journalists. "Floyd, for whatever reason, didn't want to commit," Arum said. More accurately, he said, Mayweather had chosen to ignore the proposed contract and hadn't communicated with anyone. Or could it be that Mayweather just didn't like the unilateral appeal of nature Arum and the Pacquiao camp?

Mayweather didn't bother to call by the deadline set by Arum. In fact, the usually loquacious Mayweather probably wasn't even listening. He had good reasons for not getting into the weeds of a PR campaign. His uncle and trainer Roger Mayweather was set to go on trial early on charges of assaulting and choking a female boxer. Roger Mayweather had pleaded not guilty but could face up to sixteen years in prison. He has always been a seminal influence on his nephew.

"I understand Floyd's position, regarding Roger," said Arum. "I can understand Floyd delaying until there is a resolution of the Roger situation. I don't think you guys should be too harsh on Floyd." But when asked to speculate on why Mayweather wouldn't even bother to call him and explain his reasons for bowing out of the fight of the century? "I can't figure it out," Arum admitted.

The next two days were equally strange, as the Mayweather camp seemed to wake up. Mayweather adviser Leonard Ellerbe released a statement: "Here are the facts. Al Haymon, Richard Schaefer and myself speak to each other on a regular basis and the truth is no negotiations have ever taken place nor was there ever a deal agreed upon by Team Mayweather or Floyd Mayweather to fight Manny Pacquiao on November 13. Either Ross Greenburg or Bob Arum is not telling the truth, but history tells us who is lying." Ellerbe was implying that Arum was a liar, but Greenburg was also left in a difficult position. Greenburg decided to release a statement saying that negotiations had taken place.

"Fights like Mayweather versus Pacquiao are significant because of these fighters' ability to connect with sports fans around the world," said Greenburg. "It's unfortunate that it won't happen in 2010. I had been negotiating with a representative from each side since May 2, carefully trying to put the fight together. Hopefully, someday this fight will happen. Sports fans deserve it."

Arum started trying to get another fight for Pacquiao. He settled on Antonio Margarito, who fights out of Tijuana, and is a Top Rank fighter. But Margarito was hardly a popular choice among the public, and he was finding it difficult to get a boxing license after officials confiscated "loaded" hand wraps before his failed world welterweight title defense in January 2009.

In August 2010, Margarito was denied a boxing license by the California State Athletic Commission, but he received a license in Texas, where he was set to fight Pacquiao on November 13 at Cowboys Stadium. The bout would be for the WBC super welterweight title. Pacquiao would be fighting for an unprecedented eighth world title in as many different weight divisions.

Meanwhile, promoter Don King, who once called Bob Arum a "rat fink," tried to lure Floyd Mayweather into his own stable of fighters. Both promoters said they could come to terms between Pacquiao and Mayweather for a megafight. The greatest fight ever had turned into the biggest farce in the sport's history.

Sugar Ray Leonard talks about Pacquiao fighting Mayweather, and what it would mean to the sport. "No matter what they say, ultimately, it's about bragging rights. They want the money; I wanted the money. But for the guys, it's bragging rights." Because the two men weren't forced to engage in the ring, Leonard concluded, "It's a dark period right now."

If Pacquiao and Mayweather never meet, it would be a major body blow to boxing, a sport that had been gaining mainstream momentum, mostly because of Pacquiao. It will also be a blow to both men's reputations. They are both all-time-greats but their inability to fight each other could haunt their legacies. Instead of talking about fighting each other the rest of their lives, they will be questioned why they couldn't clash in the ring. At age thirty-one, Pacquiao privately says he would like to fight a few more times, but he is a congress-man now with large responsibilities. Pacquiao will train for future fights in Manila, returning, as is his routine, to Holly-wood's Wild Card Gym for a month before his bouts. Whomever he fights, he will be shadowboxing underneath a small photo of Floyd Mayweather, imagining how he could vanquish his biggest rival.

ACKNOWLEDGMENTS

I would like to thank all of my boxing "explainers," especially Freddie Roach for allowing me to spend time in his gym, and Manny Pacquiao who let me have a glimpse into his world.

Time magazine's Howard Chua-Eoan, the *Atlantic*'s Bob Cohn, and *Esquire*'s Matt Sullivan were always supportive of this book.

Chino Trinidad, my friend, kept me alive in Sarangani and helped me in countless ways. Yobie Benjamin, another friend, gave me good advice throughout the writing of *Pac-Man*. Fred Sternburg was pivotal.

While much of this biography comes from first hand observation and reporting, the boxing coverage in the *Los Angeles Times*, ESPN, *Sports Illustrated*, *The Ring*, and Yahoo! helped inform the book. The major Filipino papers were also of great help to clarify certain events. Thank you to all of the reporters and boxing writers who answered my questions.

Thanks to Kevin Hanover, my editor at Da Capo Press, Lori Hobkirk at the Book Factory, and Michelle Tessler, my agent, extraordinary, as always.

My parents: two of the best people you could ever have in your corner.

Leslie, Rose, and Joe: I am lucky to have you.

ABOUT THE AUTHOR

Gary Andrew Poole is the author of *The Galloping Ghost*. He is a contributor to *Time*, and he has also written for the *Atlantic*, *Esquire*, and the *New York Times*. He lives in Los Angeles.